THE
FUTURE
of
GARDENS

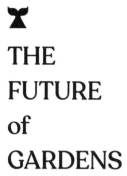

THE
FUTURE
of
GARDENS

Mark Lane

MELVILLE HOUSE UK
LONDON

THE FUTURE of GARDENS

First published in 2025 by
Melville House UK
Suite 2000
16/18 Woodford Road
London E7 0HA
and
Melville House Publishing
46 John Street
Brooklyn, NY 11201

mhpbooks.com @melvillehouse

A CIP catalogue record for this book is available from the British Library

UK ISBN: 9781911545774
US ISBN: 9781685892098

1 3 5 7 9 10 8 6 4 2

Printed in Denmark by Nørhaven, Viborg
Typesetting by Roland Codd

The authorized representative in the EU for product safety and compliance is
Easy Access System Europe, Mustamäe tee 50, 10621 Tallinn, Estonia
gpsr.requests@easproject.com

Foreword

Garden as though you will live forever
William Kent, 1685–1748, progenitor of the
naturalistic 'English Landscape'

The notion of 'forever' is an interesting one. As a garden designer, broadcaster and writer I am always told that the gardens that I design are a living legacy for generations to come. Although I don't see them in this way, it raises a very interesting point about the future of gardens and gardening. And one key question instantly springs to mind: with limited free time, smaller personal outdoor spaces and the ever-growing range of electronic, AI-generated and AI-run horticultural products that are already on the market – and will undoubtedly appear over the coming years – what role will we humans have when it comes to caring for the soil, growing on seedlings, watering, planting out and propagating? In short, will the gardening of the future all be done by machines, and gardens be devoid of humans?

Personally, I don't think it's possible to discuss the future of gardens without first dwelling a little on AI. When we think of artificial intelligence, sci-fi images and humanoid robots come to mind – or perhaps even a global network intent on killing the human race (yes, I'm a great *Terminator* fan). Perhaps, however, there are more practical matters to consider. I believe, for example, that I would embrace an AI-powered gardening assistant to inform me how to care for a plant, when it's the best time to water it, what I should be feeding it with, and how I can make more plants for free by propagating it. Surely this is something that we should welcome, whether you're a new or an experienced gardener.

There is some hesitation on my part, though. The correct information is key to proper execution, i.e. to being able to garden correctly – and learning from our mistakes can make us better gardeners. I fear that new online outlets may appear compiled solely by AI bots, who have searched the internet for every detail relating to your enquiry, and now present it succinctly. Will the information provided be correct? As a former editor, I would check all the information, but this will not always be possible, especially with our hectic lifestyles. I would hate the idea that a gardener follows a set of instructions, only to find that they have killed their plant(s) because the wrong material has been disseminated.

Similarly, sensors in gardens linked to computers – in other words, a 'Smart Garden' – can help gardeners understand how we respond to plants: when they need irrigation, how we take in and interact with the different aspects of a garden, or whether we walk straight through the outdoor space. Lines of data are built, which, in turn, increases the AI knowledge. This is not just helpful for tending gardens, but also for designing them. But while artificial intelligence *can* design gardens, the question is whether it *should*. For me as a garden designer and gardener, the personal touch, getting to know the client and their aspirations, is essential to creating an accessible and inclusive design that works for them perfectly. Losing the human element will, in my opinion, make the process dry and sterile. We also know that gardening is beneficial for our physical and mental well-being, so I would hate to see a time when AI and robots do all the work.

Another exciting prospect is the integration of AI in plant breeding. By analysing genetic data, AI algorithms could identify desirable traits and predict the potential success of specific plant hybrids. This could accelerate the development of new plant varieties with enhanced resistance to pests, diseases and environmental stressors, contributing to more resilient and sustainable gardens. And, with our ever-changing climate, such traits will be essential. And it's not just individual plots that potentially stand to benefit from this innovation. The gardening and horticulture industries are enormous: it's not just about digging a hole in the ground and planting something; it incorporates the perfume industry, seed cloning, farming, floriculture, landscaping, agribusiness, agrochemicals, packaging, cold storage and so much more. All of these sectors are already and will, in my opinion, *increasingly* embrace AI-powered products to maximise output, assist with day-to-day operations and production lines, and ultimately increase their financial returns.

What a fascinating thing the garden of the future could be – and, in some cases, already is: intelligent devices and sensors, seamlessly integrated and continuously monitoring environmental conditions and plant health, are already in use. Smart-irrigation systems, for instance, are designed to analyse real-time weather data, soil moisture levels and plants' requirements to optimise watering schedules. This not only conserves water but also ensures that plants receive the precise amount they need for optimal growth. AI-driven robotic lawnmowers autonomously navigate through the garden, maintaining the perfect grass height without human intervention. And with the ability to process vast amounts of data related to plant species, soil types, climate conditions and aesthetic preferences, AI algorithms could assist garden designers like me in creating bespoke plans tailored to each client's unique requirements. This could streamline the design process, providing more accurate predictions of how different plants will thrive in specific environments and freeing me up to do other things, such as keeping the lines of communication with the client open and ensuring they are regularly updated.

In the realm of garden education and community building, AI-powered platforms have the potential to foster a richer online experience for enthusiasts. Just think of a virtual gardening community where individuals could connect, share experiences and seek advice – we're already seeing this to some extent on social media. AI could further facilitate personalised content recommendations, making learning about gardening more accessible and tailoring it to individual interests. My main concern is who will police this dissemination of material. Inevitably, it will be down to the gardener, designer, scientist or researcher to fact-check at every stage – something that I already urge all designers and gardeners to do.

I believe it's true that we are living through unprecedented times. The rate at which the internet, science, medicine, electronics, AI and even cloning are growing is both fascinating and concerning. I love modern technology and how it can assist us in carrying out work quicker and more efficiently, but I still remember the days before mobile phones, apps, social media and small electronic devices that you can hold in your hand to change lighting schemes, turn on your washing machine or watch how much electricity you're using. The idea of electric cars when I was a small boy was science fiction and yet, in my lifetime, I know we shall see more of these cars on the road. I have already joined the electric car 'club', and with improved battery life and range, it will soon be easy to drive from one end of the UK to the other, with spare battery power, on a single charge. Science fiction is here already.

Yet it's crucial to approach the integration of AI in gardening with a mindful and ethical perspective. As we embrace these amazing technological advances, it's essential to balance innovation with environmental sustainability and biodiversity. Additionally, ensuring that AI tools remain accessible and user-friendly is key to understanding the benefits of these technologies across diverse demographics. If we can manage all of this, the future of gardening is exciting and filled with possibilities. From smart systems optimising garden maintenance, to personalised design and community-building platforms, the potential for positive transformation is vast.

A Unique Perspective

I started gardening at a very young age. I used to follow my grandparents around their gardens, watching and learning all the time. On my father's side, I would follow my grandfather, dragging around a blue-painted trolley containing a blunt pair of scissors, a ball of string and packets of seeds, as he taught me about caring for the soil (a quite unique approach during the 1970s, when chemical pesticides and herbicides were at the forefront of gardening), how to sow seeds, propagating plants, tying in and so much more. My grandmother, who was a flower arranger for the local Women's Institute, taught me about colour, texture, shape and form. One of my earliest memories was, as a six-year-old boy, cutting some chrysanthemums from the garden and running indoors to watch my grandmother arrange them in a large cut-glass vase with lots of foliage, also taken from the garden.

On my mother's side, my grandparents' garden was full of bush roses, and as a young boy with my older brother, all we wanted to do was play in the garden, roll on the lawn and see what shapes we could see in the clouds above. But my grandmother made us squish green- and blackflies between our fingertips and pick up leaves that may have had black spots on them. At the time, I didn't really think that I was being taught about gardening and nature, but now these happy memories stick with me.

I grew up in the late sixties and seventies in an apartment in Hove, on the south-east coast of England near Brighton. From one side of the apartment, we looked over the South Downs, a range of chalk hills, and on the other the sea, the English Channel. We had a small communal garden and I remember one day asking my mother if we could plant up around a solitary rose in a circular border. We bought some plants from the local grocer's store (garden centres were only just appearing on our streets), took them home and planted them. By the end of the year, each of the twelve apartments had its own section of border that they maintained while the garden maintenance company came in, mowed the lawns and pruned the shrubs and trees. This community spirit was fun, engaging and informative. I would go out there, chat with a neighbour who was in his eighties, learn about his childhood and why gardening was important to him, and then the following day chat to a housewife who was growing rhubarb and picking it to make rhubarb crumble. Every summer holiday was special and different, and I relished them.

When I left home to study art history at University College London, my love and interest in gardening were put to one side; however, I did become fascinated by landscape architecture, how buildings relate to the natural environment and how this is depicted in art (something that is important to my work today as a garden designer). Having finished my degree, I became an editor. Initially I worked on medical publications, but I soon started work for an arts publisher, then became the Publishing Director for the Royal Institute of British Architects (RIBA); and finally the Managing Editor for the international arts publisher Thames & Hudson. While Publishing Director for RIBA I worked with many landscape architects. I had also met my husband by this point, and our first home in south-east London had a small garden, which I loved (each time we moved, the garden got bigger). My passion for plants and gardening and everything horticultural grew. While I worked at Thames & Hudson, producing stunning publications, we published numerous gardening books; every waking moment I would read about plants.

Then, in 2000, I was in a serious car crash. Being born with spina bifida meant that, unfortunately, I would lose the feeling in my legs, and I started a new life as a wheelchair user. During my long rehabilitation, I worked with a horticultural therapist, who, along with my husband, suggested that perhaps I should consider leaving the publishing world and finding a job in the gardening industry, as I had an 'encyclopaedic brain' for plants. It wasn't until I finally got home, after twelve months of rehabilitation in the hospital, that the idea became a reality. I looked for online courses, found the right one for me, and studied garden design.

The intervening twenty-four years have been enormous fun – I have genuinely loved every minute of it. Being the UK's first garden designer in a wheelchair gives me a unique perspective: I remember how I used to look at plants and borders from a standing position, but now I get to see the garden up close and personal, and I focus on accessibility and inclusive design, without creating spaces that look boring and institutional.

In 2015, I started writing for the horticultural press, and one of my articles was seen by a researcher from the BBC for the programme *Gardeners' World*. They asked me if I would be interested in doing a piece to camera, which I did one cold afternoon in our back garden. I thought nothing would come of it – this was my five minutes of fame. Yet shortly afterwards I was asked to present at the Royal Horticultural Society (RHS) Chelsea Flower Show. I loved the experience and quietly wished to do more. Fortunately, my dream was realised: I became one of the new presenters for *Gardeners' World* and the RHS shows. Using my plant and gardening knowledge and experience, I then started a new chapter as the garden expert on the BBC's *Morning Live*, which I still do today and which I love being part of, and for QVC, the home shopping network where I have my own shows. (Unfortunately, my love for gardens, gardening and plants could not be put to good use when I appeared on *Celebrity Mastermind*, *Pointless Celebrities* or *Celebrity Weakest Link*!)

Gardening is so different now, and when I look back at what I had to hand growing up in the seventies, eighties and nineties, compared to what is available these days, it feels like we have made great advances. Smart technology already helps me on a day-to-day basis. For example, as a garden designer, I now use a drone to capture footage and shots of new areas to design – especially useful when I'm designing a ten-acre garden, or when I cannot get into some parts of the landscape because of the rough terrain. Laser levels and smart measuring devices enable me to capture the landscape in 3D, which I can then import into my computer software to start designing. Apps on my phone enable me to check plant identifications, the aspect of the landscape, the terrain and so much more. My phone has also become my camera for filming myself, and with the use of portable lighting, a personal autocue system and microphones, I can set myself up anywhere and either pre-record or shoot live to the studio. And Google Maps has helped me when writing books: when I wrote *Royal Gardens of the World*[*], I was able to 'walk' through most of the gardens before visiting them, so I could work out accessible routes. Many of these devices were once for professional use only, but with the advent of cheaper products and the ever-changing electronics market, anybody can now

---

[*] Kyle Books, Kyle Cathie Ltd (Hachette), 2020.

buy off-the-shelf items that were seen as the stuff of science fiction – or were, at least, prohibitively expensive – only twenty years ago.

The use of personal devices can only go a short way to changing everyday activities. I find it interesting and exciting what the future might hold for me as a garden designer, broadcaster and writer, but I strongly believe that garden design needs a human element, in addition to such devices. This personal approach makes all the difference: a lot of the time it's what clients *don't* say that reveals the potential for their new garden. AI and smart technologies, currently, are largely unable to pick up on this silent element.

During my rehabilitation, I met some incredible groups and individuals who are making a huge difference within the disability and horticultural fields. As a result, I now work closely with many charities that use gardening and social and therapeutic horticulture (STH) to positively change lives. We know from the research that gardening is beneficial for our mental and physical well-being: one of the largest studies to date on gardens and gardening, from the National Institute for Health Research in the United Kingdom, found that people who spend time in the garden report better physical and mental health levels than those who do not garden.[†] Similar research carried out by the UK's King's Fund also found reductions in depression and anxiety, and improved social functioning.[‡] This bio-philic response (our innate need to be surrounded by nature) is strong.

We know that, when in contact with skin on our hands, beneficial *Mycobacterium vaccae*, which occurs naturally in soil, releases the feel-good chemicals serotonin and endorphins in the brain. People who exercise – and this includes gardening – have up to a 35 per cent lower risk of coronary heart disease and stroke, and thirty minutes of gardening are equivalent to playing a session of badminton or volleyball, or practising yoga. Gardening provides a low-impact form of exercise, promoting flexibility and strength. Like walking in nature or forest-bathing, just sitting in the garden or outdoors surrounded by nature can help lower blood pressure with countless reports of people feeling calmer

---

† Siân de Bell, Mathew White, Alistair Griffiths, Alison Darlow, Timothy Taylor, Benedict Wheeler, Rebecca Lovell, 'Spending time in the garden is positively associated with health and well-being: Results from a national survey in England', *Landscape and Urban Planning*, Volume 200, 2020.

‡ David Buck, The King's Fund, 'Gardens and health: Implications for policy and practice'. Report commissioned by the National Gardens Scheme, May 2016.

and more relaxed. Exposure to natural elements and green spaces has been associated with reduced levels of the stress hormone cortisol and enhanced feelings of well-being. So, whether you're an active or passive gardener, you can reap an immeasurable sense of well-being.

I know this all too well. During my stay in hospital, I loved getting outside. As soon as I was in the garden my shoulders dropped, my breathing slowed down and I felt more relaxed. Today, when weeding, my mind starts to wander as an act of mindfulness. I know what's going on around me, but getting my bare hands in the soil makes me feel better, grounded and at one with nature, diverting my attention from everyday stressors. Watching seeds sprout, plants grow and flowers bloom provide a tangible sense of achievement. Completing gardening tasks, whether small or large, instils a sense of purpose and accomplishment in me, and this positive reinforcement boosts my self-esteem and contributes to a positive outlook on life. Without gardening and nature, I would certainly be a different person today.

Without smart technology and AI, I don't think my own life would change dramatically, although the ability to buy products through my smart speaker or to listen to my favourite music with a few verbal commands would be missed. Yet there are changes afoot that have the potential to revolutionise gardening, making it more inclusive and accessible, not just for disabled people, but for everyone.

Smart Gardening, Smart Cities and Sustainable Gardening Practices

Smart gardening and technological innovation can help redefine how we approach and experience horticulture, gardening and the joy of cultivating plants. By using the power of interconnected devices, it is becoming increasingly possible to develop more efficient, sustainable and user-friendly gardening practices.

At the heart of the smart gardening revolution are intelligent systems that continuously collect data from various sources within the garden environment and analyse it within milliseconds. These sources include weather conditions, soil moisture levels, sunlight exposure, and even the specific needs of individual plant species. The bit we don't see, the integration of AI algorithms, allows for the processing of this data in real time, enabling smart gardening systems to make informed decisions and execute precise actions. This might sound like science fiction, but there are already smart watering systems that can be bought online or in store that analyse the data, making it easier for the gardener or commercial grower. Link this to your phone, with useful apps, and you can care for your plants whether you're in the garden, in the polytunnel or away on holiday, sunning yourself and drinking a cocktail.

One of the primary applications of smart gardening is irrigation. Traditional watering systems often rely on predetermined schedules, which may not align with the dynamic needs of different plants. Smart irrigation systems, on the other hand, use AI to assess environmental conditions and plant requirements. Link this up with an automated feeding station and the right nutrients can be given to the plants at the correct dosage for optimal growth. An excellent example is the use of precision irrigation in Israel, in the Negev Desert, where scarcity of water is a persistent challenge. The country's innovative drip irrigation systems, such as small irrigation tubes with water sprinklers linked to a timer, ensure that water is targeted directly at the root zones of plants, maximising efficiency and conserving this precious resource. This technology has not only transformed agricultural productivity but also serves as a model for water-efficient gardening in arid regions globally. It might come as a surprise that 70 per cent of the world's water goes to agriculture, but Netafirm in Israel has worked out that to cultivate crops in desert regions, they had to grow more for less. With the use of drip irrigation, which was invented in 1959, water can be conserved. Sensors have been placed in the soil to understand what the plant needs. Also, some tech-savvy individuals in Israel created the 'Croptune' app, where the gardener or grower can take a picture of a plant and get an instant analysis of its requirements, such as nutrients. The end result is that Israel has achieved self-sufficiency in the face of adversity.§

Robotic lawnmowers represent another facet of smart gardening now in mainstream use. AI-driven navigation systems can cross the garden terrain efficiently. Equipped with sensors, they can detect obstacles and adjust their path accordingly, providing a hands-free solution to lawn maintenance. This not only saves time and effort for gardeners but also contributes to a consistently manicured lawn – something the English are very proud of. (Though, while it's lovely

§ Ministry of Economy and Industry, Israëlissche Handelsmissie in Nederland, 'Innovative Israeli irrigation technology to tackle climate change', 30 May 2024.

to see a well-manicured, mown lawn with stripes, they may not be to everyone's taste: in my opinion, a 'wilder' lawn not only requires less water but is alive with wildlife.) The tech involved, however, has been applied on a larger scale for some time already: the tractors I see where I live in rural Lincolnshire are now manoeuvred around fields using sensors.

In contemporary agriculture, tractors have evolved into sophisticated machines that incorporate advanced technologies, including sensors and geo-location systems. Such innovations represent a significant leap forward in enhancing efficiency, precision and sustainability in farming practices, and are helping to reshape the agricultural landscape. Sensors gather real-time data from the field, providing farmers with valuable insights to optimise their operations. Global Positioning System (GPS) technology enables precise tracking of the tractor's location within the field, allowing them to navigate fields with minimal overlap and optimal precision, often with no operator or driver inside – a technology that we see now in robotic mowers.

This not only reduces fuel consumption but also enhances the uniformity of tasks such as planting and harvesting. And when tractors can be 'electrified', just like electric mowers, the need for carbon-based fuel will be removed. Variable Rate Technology (VRT) uses geo-location data to adjust the application rates of inputs, such as fertilisers and pesticides, based on specific field conditions. This targeted approach ensures that resources are applied where they are needed most, reducing waste and environmental impact. Geo-location technology helps with the creation of accurate field maps and boundaries. Farmers can therefore plan and organise their operations with precision, ensuring that every inch of the field is used effectively. Imagine this being transferred to the domestic outdoor setting, where every inch of the garden, allotment, community garden or roof terrace can be utilised to maximise efficiency – essential if growing your food can lead to self-sufficiency.

These developments in agriculture clearly point the way for what we might see in technology for the garden, potentially at an even more precise level. Another example is the use of soil sensors: on farms, these are deployed to measure various parameters, including moisture levels, nutrient content and temperature. This data allows farmers to make informed decisions about irrigation, fertiliser application and overall soil health management. Weather sensors monitor atmospheric conditions, providing real-time data on temperature, humidity and precipitation. This information aids farmers in making timely decisions, such as adjusting planting schedules or preparing for adverse weather events. Integrated camera systems capture high-resolution images of the field, which can then be analysed to inspect crop health, detect pests or diseases and assess overall crop performance.

As gardeners, or stewards of the land, we too need to consider minimising our environmental impact – and some smart gardening devices already include sensors that monitor soil conditions and nutrient levels, just like those found in commercial farming machines. This AI-driven, personalised approach to plant care will surely enhance the overall health and vitality of the gardens of the future.

ı ⟩ ⟩ ▶ ▶ ▶

The integration of smart gardening technologies has the potential to extend beyond individual garden plots. Smart city initiatives are exploring the incorporation of green spaces with intelligent systems to create more sustainable urban environments. Green roofs and living walls equipped with sensors can contribute to energy efficiency by regulating temperature, capturing rainwater and promoting biodiversity within urban landscapes, while helping to reduce the 'heat island' effect. A city heat island (also known as an urban heat island) refers to the phenomenon where urban areas experience significantly higher temperatures than their surrounding rural areas, due to materials and surfaces, lack of vegetation, building density and height, excess energy use and air pollution. Yet, as with any technological advance, ethical considerations must be taken into account. Balancing the benefits of smart gardening with environmental sustainability, data privacy and accessibility is paramount. Ensuring that these technologies remain user-friendly and adaptable to diverse gardening practices is crucial for their widespread adoption and positive impact. In essence, smart gardening represents a compelling fusion of nature and technology, where AI serves as a valuable ally in the pursuit of cultivating vibrant, resilient and aesthetically pleasing outdoor spaces. As technology continues to advance, the future of smart gardening holds the promise of even more sophisticated, intuitive and eco-friendly solutions for gardeners and garden enthusiasts alike.

Another indicator of the technologies that may soon be available to gardeners can be found in 'smart cities'. This concept, which I will discuss in more detail later, represents a transformative approach to urban living, where technology and data-driven solutions are harnessed to enhance efficiency, sustainability and the overall quality of life for residents. Smart cities use a variety of technologies, including the Internet of Things (IoT), data analytics and AI, to optimise infrastructure, services and resource management.

The notion of the Internet of Things has gained momentum over the past decade, altering the way we interact with the world around us and reshaping our understanding of how devices and systems interact. It involves connecting everyday physical objects to the internet, allowing them to collect, exchange and act upon data without requiring human intervention. This interconnected network of devices includes everything from household appliances and wearable fitness trackers to industrial machines and city infrastructure. Fundamentally, IoT uses devices and sensors to collect data from their surroundings, just like the aforementioned AI farming technology. Once data is collected, it needs to be sent somewhere for analysis. IoT devices use various communication methods to connect to the internet, including Wi-Fi, Bluetooth, cellular networks or specialised communication protocols like Zigbee or LoRaWAN. This connectivity enables the devices to transmit data to cloud-based servers or directly to other devices. The data collected is often processed either in the cloud or on the device itself (the latter is known as edge computing). Cloud computing allows for complex data analysis, utilising powerful servers to process large datasets and apply machine learning algorithms or other advanced analytics. In contrast, edge computing processes data locally, which is particularly useful for time-sensitive tasks that require immediate action, such as plant care and gardening. After the data is processed, the information is presented to the user in a meaningful way. This could be through a mobile app, a web dashboard, or even automated actions taken by the device without direct user interaction. For instance, a smart irrigation system might automatically water plants when soil moisture levels drop below a certain threshold, with the user only receiving periodic updates on the system's status.

But what are the advantages of IoT? Efficiency and automation come to mind. Also, the data generated by IoT devices provides valuable insights that can inform better decision-making. It can also lead to substantial cost reductions in areas such as energy consumption, maintenance and operational efficiency. In the home, IoT devices enhance comfort, convenience and security.

Despite its many benefits, IoT also presents challenges that need to be addressed, such as security risks. Because IoT devices are connected to the internet, they can be vulnerable to cyberattacks. Ensuring that these devices are secure is critical. IoT devices collect vast amounts of data, raising questions about who owns this data and how it is used. Of course, with a wide variety of devices from different manufacturers, ensuring that all IoT devices can communicate effectively with one another is a challenge. A lack of standardisation will hinder the development and deployment of IoT systems.

The future of IoT is full of potential, then, with several trends likely to shape its development: 5G technology, AI integration, a shift towards locally processed data (rather than sending it to the cloud), and sustainability initiatives such as reducing energy consumption, managing natural resources more efficiently and minimising waste.

The Internet of Things is revolutionising how we interact with technology and the world around us. By enabling devices to communicate and make decisions autonomously, IoT offers a level of efficiency, convenience and insight that was previously unimaginable. However, as IoT continues to evolve, it will be essential to address challenges related to security, privacy and interoperability to fully realise its potential. As these issues are resolved, IoT is likely to become an even more integral part of our daily lives, driving innovation across a wide range of industries and creating a more connected, intelligent world.

Gardens can never be seen as independent entities. They sit within a larger environment, often busy urban settings, and with more connectivity than ever before, understanding how the larger space relates to our small defined gardens is essential. This is why it's so important to understand smart cities. 'These focus on creating *intelligent (world) infrastructure* that responds dynamically to the needs of the community. For instance, smart traffic management systems utilise real-time data from sensors and cameras to optimise traffic flow, reduce congestion and enhance overall transport efficiency. Singapore's Smart Nation initiative is a good example, where the city-state employs a comprehensive network of sensors, cameras and data analytics to monitor and manage traffic in real time.

Smart cities prioritise *sustainable energy solutions* to reduce environmental impact and promote resource efficiency. Copenhagen in Denmark stands out as a global leader in this regard. The city has integrated smart grids, renewable energy sources and energy-efficient technologies, creating a more sustainable and resilient energy infrastructure. Smart meters and sensors enable residents to monitor and control their energy consumption, contributing to overall energy conservation. This is one reason why the United Kingdom recently physically linked up to the integrated smart grids in Denmark to reach net zero carbon emissions by 2050.

Going one step further is Seoul, in South Korea, which has embraced technology to provide seamless public services. The city's *smart governance initiatives* include online platforms for citizen engagement, smart healthcare services and integrated public transportation systems. These efforts enhance the overall quality of life for residents while promoting transparency and citizen participation in decision-making processes. Smart cities emphasise environmental monitoring to address challenges related to pollution, waste management and green spaces. Amsterdam, in the Netherlands, has implemented a range of smart solutions to promote environmental sustainability. Smart waste management systems use sensors to optimise waste collection routes, reducing fuel consumption and minimising environmental impact. Additionally, the city employs green roofs and smart irrigation systems to enhance urban biodiversity and reduce the urban heat island effect.

Smart cities are being set up to prioritise the safety and well-being of their residents through advanced technologies. In Barcelona, Spain, the implementation of IoT devices and data analytics has led to improved public safety. Smart street lighting is a good example: it not only reduces energy consumption, but also serves as a network for environmental sensors and surveillance cameras. This interconnected infrastructure enhances security, making public spaces less dangerous for residents and visitors.

Ensuring digital inclusion and accessibility is another key aspect of the smart city experience. For instance, in Vienna, Austria, the Smart City Wien framework focuses on creating an inclusive digital environment. The city provides digital services for citizens of all ages and backgrounds, promoting equal access to technology and information. This approach contributes to a more connected and empowered community and, in turn, a community with better mental and physical health and well-being.

Smart cities therefore represent a forward-thinking approach to urban development, employing technology to create more efficient, sustainable and liveable environments. While each smart city initiative is tailored to the unique needs of its community, the overarching goal is to harness innovation to address urban challenges and improve the overall quality of life for residents – and green spaces are part of this initiative. By looking at the implementation of smart cities, the future of gardening with IoT holds tremendous potential to transform the way we interact with and nurture our outdoor spaces. The integration of smart technologies not only optimises resource usage and enhances plant health but also fosters a more connected and informed gardening community. As these innovations continue to evolve, gardeners can look forward to a future where technology and nature harmoniously coexist, contributing to the creation of thriving and sustainable gardens and landscapes.

The relationship between smart technologies and sustainability is an interesting one. In fact, smart technologies have become integral in promoting sustainable gardening practices worldwide, offering innovative solutions to environmental challenges, optimising resource utilisation and enhancing the overall eco-friendliness of gardening. As mentioned earlier, smart technologies contribute to sustainable urban gardening through the implementation of green roof systems. Cities like Singapore are leveraging green roof technology to enhance energy efficiency, reduce urban heat islands and promote biodiversity. Smart sensors monitor the moisture levels of the green roofs, optimising irrigation and ensuring that the vegetation thrives. This not only beautifies urban landscapes but also provides insulation, improving energy efficiency in buildings.

Efficient waste management is a crucial aspect of sustainable gardening. Automated composting systems, integrated with smart sensors, facilitate the decomposition of organic waste into nutrient-rich compost. Amsterdam uses community-based composting initiatives with smart technology to monitor and optimise the composting process. This not only diverts organic waste from landfill but also produces valuable compost for community gardens, closing the loop on the nutrient cycle.

Smart technologies are fostering community engagement in sustainable gardening practices. The Grow Observatory project in Europe is a notable example: here citizen scientists use sensors to collect and share data on soil health and climate conditions. This collaborative effort empowers individuals to make informed decisions about sustainable gardening practices while contributing to a broader understanding of environmental patterns. AI is being employed to promote biodiversity and sustainability in urban landscaping projects. In Barcelona, AI algorithms analyse environmental data to recommend the most suitable plant species for public spaces. This approach not only enhances the resilience of urban flora but also reduces the need for excessive water, herbicides, pesticides and other chemicals.

The integration of solar-powered smart devices in gardening helps reduce reliance on conventional energy sources. In Australia, where sunlight is abundant, solar-powered sensors and irrigation systems are employed in sustainable gardening practices. These devices harness solar energy to power sensors that monitor soil conditions and control irrigation, minimising the environmental impact associated with energy consumption.

On a micro scale, but with a macro effect, smartphone applications are empowering gardeners worldwide to adopt sustainable practices. Apps like 'Smart Plant' and 'GardenTags' provide users with information on eco-friendly gardening practices, plant selection based on local conditions and tips for water conservation. These applications help contribute to a global movement promoting sustainable gardening practices accessible to both novice and experienced gardeners. Smart technologies are therefore already playing a pivotal role in advancing sustainable gardening practices across the globe, and this will only increase as the technologies advance. From precision irrigation to community-driven initiatives and AI-enhanced plant selection, these innovations contribute to more efficient resource usage, reduced environmental impact and the creation of resilient and vibrant gardens. As technology continues to evolve, the integration of smart solutions in gardening will likely play an even more significant role in fostering sustainable and environmentally conscious practices.

The Climate Crisis

Every day in the news we see the effects of climate change: flooding, droughts, increased temperatures across the planet, lost environments and ecosystems. In the future, gardens and gardening will have to live with the climate crisis. In the United Kingdom, gardeners are noticing shifts in traditional planting times due to milder winters and warmer springs. This has led to the exploration of new plant varieties that are better suited to the changing climate, ensuring successful cultivation despite altered growing conditions. In fact, the UK is increasingly

looking to collaborate with international partners
to address the challenges posed by extreme weather,
such as heavy rainfall, floods, heatwaves and storms,
which are becoming more frequent and severe.
The UK is a signatory to the Paris Agreement, has
taken a leadership role in the annual United Nations
Climate Change Conference (COP) and is engaging
in bilateral and multilateral partnerships to enhance
its ability to respond to extreme weather. However,
we are not alone.

The Netherlands is implementing green infrastructure initiatives in urban areas to enhance
biodiversity. Community gardens, green roofs and
urban green spaces are designed to support local
ecosystems and provide habitats for pollinators,
contributing to the preservation of biodiversity in
the face of urbanisation and climate change. Costa
Rica, known for its commitment to environmental
conservation, encourages agroforestry practices
that integrate trees and crops. This approach not
only enhances carbon sequestration but also promotes sustainable farming, demonstrating the
potential of gardening and agriculture in mitigating climate change. Traditional crops are becoming
less viable in parts of India that are experiencing
more intense heatwaves. Farmers and gardeners are

experimenting with heat-tolerant crop varieties, such as drought-resistant millets, to adapt to the changing climate and ensure food security. Sustainable farming practices in Brazil, such as agroecology and agroforestry, focus on improving soil health. By incorporating cover crops (plants grown primarily to improve and protect soil health rather than for harvest), rotating crops and minimising chemical inputs, these practices enhance soil resilience and contribute to climate adaptation in the agricultural sector. In Japan, where typhoons are common, gardeners have developed resilient garden designs. Features like windbreaks, raised beds and improved drainage help gardens withstand extreme weather events. This approach ensures that gardens can recover more quickly after storms and continue to thrive. Educational programmes in Canada promote sustainable gardening practices to address the impact of climate change on local ecosystems. Workshops and community initiatives teach gardeners about native plant species, composting and water conservation, fostering a community-wide understanding of the role that gardens play in climate resilience.

In Italy, the Slow Food movement encourages the consumption of locally grown, seasonal produce. Community Supported Agriculture (CSA) initiatives

connect consumers directly with local farmers
and gardeners, promoting a more sustainable and
climate-resilient food system. And the gardening
community in South Africa actively participates in
initiatives that promote climate action. Gardening
clubs and environmental organisations collaborate
to advocate for policies that address climate change,
showcasing the role of individual gardeners in
larger-scale efforts to combat the climate crisis.

These are just a few examples that illustrate the
diverse ways in which gardeners worldwide are
adapting to the challenges posed by the climate
crisis. By embracing sustainable practices, experimenting with new plant varieties and advocating
for broader climate action, gardeners can contribute
not only to the resilience of their own gardens but
also to a macro-level, collective effort to mitigate the
impacts of a changing climate.

Resilient Gardening

Resilient gardening in the face of climate challenges
involves adopting practices and strategies that enhance
a garden's ability to withstand and adapt to changing
environmental conditions. This approach recognises
the impact of climate change on traditional gardening
practices and seeks to build gardens that are robust,

sustainable and better equipped to thrive. Resilient gardens prioritise diversity in plant selection. This includes choosing varieties of plant species that are adapted to different climatic conditions, soil types and microenvironments. Diverse plantings increase the garden's resilience by ensuring that some species are better equipped to withstand specific challenges. As the world experiences shifts in temperature, precipitation patterns and extreme weather events, gardeners globally are recognising the importance of cultivating a varied palette of plant species. This diversity not only ensures aesthetic richness but also bolsters the garden's ability to adapt.

Singapore, known for its tropical climate, has implemented a diverse plant selection strategy in Bishan-Ang Mo Kio Park. This urban green space incorporates a variety of plant species, including native and exotic plants. The diverse palette of plants not only enhances the park's visual appeal but also contributes to ecological resilience, creating habitats for a wide range of flora and fauna.

Kew Gardens in London, renowned for its botanical collections, showcases the importance of diverse plant selection. With over 30,000 different kinds of plants, Kew serves as a global hub for plant diversity conservation. Its extensive collection enables researchers and horticulturists to study and preserve a wide array of plant species, emphasising the significance of biodiversity for climate resilience.

Dr Jane Goodall, a renowned primatologist and conservationist, underlines the interconnectivity of all living things in ecosystems. In her view, diverse plant selection is fundamental not only for the resilience of gardens but for the health of the planet as a whole. She states: 'Biodiversity starts in the distant past and it points toward the future.'[¶] Professor David Tilman, an ecology and biodiversity expert, known for his research on the relationship between biodiversity and ecosystem stability, highlights the role of plant diversity in ecological resilience. His work states that diverse plant communities are more productive and resistant to environmental stressors. In gardening, this principle translates to enhanced resistance to pests, diseases and climate variations[**].

But why does diverse plant selection matter? In short, it ensures that a garden is better equipped to

---

¶ Nibandh Vinod, 'International Day for Biological Diversity 2023: Theme, History, Significance, and Quotes', New Delhi, India, News 18. ** David Tilman, Peter B. Reich and Johannes M. H. Knops, J.M.H, *Biodiversity and ecosystem stability in a decade-long grassland experiment*, Nature 441, 2006, pp. 629–632; or Tilman, D, *Biodiversity: Population Versus Ecosystem Stability*, Ecological Society of America, Volume 77, Issue 2, March 1996.

handle fluctuations in temperature and precipitation, and extreme weather events. Some plant species may thrive in warmer conditions, while others may be more resistant to drought. This diversity acts as a natural buffer against the unpredictability of climate change. A variety of plant species also disrupts the life cycle of pests and diseases, reducing the risk of widespread infestations. Monoculture, or the cultivation of a single plant species, can make gardens more susceptible to the rapid spread of pests. Diverse plantings create a less favourable environment for pests, promoting natural pest control. Diverse gardens also contribute to the enhancement of ecosystems. Different plant species attract a variety of pollinators, beneficial insects and birds. This biodiversity not only supports local ecosystems but also aids in the pollination of crops, promoting food security. As climate conditions evolve, certain plant species may become more or less suitable for a particular region. Diverse plant selection allows gardeners to adapt to these changes by introducing and experimenting with new varieties. This adaptability is crucial for maintaining garden vitality in the face of a dynamic climate.

Beyond practical considerations, diverse plantings contribute to the aesthetic appeal of gardens.

Different colours, shapes and textures create visually engaging landscapes. While diverse plant selection is vital for the creation of resilient gardens, it also presents challenges. Invasive species and habitat loss can threaten biodiversity. Gardeners need to be mindful when choosing plants to avoid introducing species that may become invasive and outcompete native flora. Incorporating native plants and those adapted to the local climate enhances a garden's resilience. Native plants are typically well-suited to the specific conditions of the region, requiring less intervention in terms of water, fertiliser and pest control. These plants have evolved to thrive in the local ecosystem. The strategic use of native and climate-adapted plants, therefore, stands out as a key pillar of resilient gardening and the future of gardens and gardening. As global temperatures rise and weather patterns become increasingly unpredictable, this approach will enhance a garden's ability to withstand climate-related stressors while contributing to broader conservation efforts. In Australia, where arid conditions and water scarcity are prevalent, the promotion of native and drought-tolerant plants is evident in bush gardens. These gardens often feature iconic Australian species such as eucalyptus, banksia and kangaroo paw. Embracing native flora conserves water and supports local ecosystems, providing habitats for native wildlife.

Xeriscape Gardens

Facing persistent drought conditions, California has seen a surge in the popularity of 'xeriscape' gardens. These gardens utilise climate-adapted plants well suited to the state's semi-arid environment. Succulents, Californian poppies and native grasses are commonly integrated into xeriscape designs, reducing water consumption and promoting ecological resilience. As temperatures rise across the planet and rainfall becomes more erratic, I believe we'll see more xeriscape gardens appearing in the future, both here in the UK and further afield.

Xeriscape gardening fascinates me, as I'm planning to introduce its fundamentals into our new garden in north Lincolnshire. A term coined from the Greek word *xeros* meaning dry, it represents a sustainable and water-efficient approach to landscaping. In regions facing water scarcity and increasingly unpredictable climatic conditions, xeriscape gardening has emerged as a mindful and ecologically responsible practice. As mentioned above, xeriscape gardens feature plants that are naturally suited to the region's climate. Drought-tolerant species, native plants and those with low water requirements take centre stage, creating a resilient and sustainable landscape. Drip irrigation, soaker hoses and other water-efficient irrigation systems help deliver water directly to the root zone, minimising wastage through evaporation or runoff. Of course, choosing plants that can survive prolonged periods of drought will ideally mean that reliance on water through soaker hoses, etc., will be diminished. The result will, therefore, often be lower water bills and reduced maintenance costs. Once established, these landscapes require less ongoing care, making them a cost-effective and sustainable choice for homeowners and communities.

Mulching plays a crucial role in xeriscape gardens by reducing the evaporation of soil moisture, suppressing weed growth and regulating soil temperature. Stone and gravel are often used, but organic mulches, such as bark or compost, contribute to the overall health of the garden. Healthy soil is fundamental for contemporary and future gardening. Amending the soil with organic matter enhances its water retention capacity and improves the availability of nutrients to plants. Well-aerated soil also promotes the development of robust root systems.

For those of you who like a lawn, xeriscape principles recommend using drought-tolerant grass varieties and minimising the size of turfed areas. This ensures that water is used efficiently and that the landscape remains resilient during dry periods. The idea of tapestry lawns also plays an important part. By selecting differing plants with similar growth patterns and drought resilience, a colourful and textural lawn can be added that requires no additional watering, little maintenance other than a trim at the end of the flowering season and minimal weeding as the dense prostrate plants block out sunlight, keeping weed growth to a minimum. Thoughtful garden design is a hallmark of xeriscape gardening. Grouping plants with similar water needs, creating focal points and incorporating hard landscaping such as rocks or pathways contribute to an aesthetically pleasing and water-efficient layout.

In addition, to design a xeriscape garden, you need to understand the climate and microclimates of your garden or region. Select plants that are well-suited to local conditions, considering factors such as temperature, sunlight and soil type. Choose plants that have evolved to thrive in arid conditions. Go around your local area and the countryside nearby and see what's growing in the hedgerows, the fields and other people's gardens. Remember to select a mix of plants that provide interest throughout the seasons, including those with attractive foliage, flowers, seedheads or berries. This will ensure that the garden remains visually appealing year-round. Regularly monitor the garden for signs of stress or overwatering. Finally, if using drip irrigation, adjust irrigation schedules based on seasonal changes and the specific needs of the plants.

Native And Climate-Adapted Plants

Doug Tallamy, an entomologist and conservationist, renowned for his work on the importance of native plants for biodiversity, emphasises the role of native plants in supporting local ecosystems. In his book *Bringing Nature Home*, he mentions that they are crucial for sustaining insect populations, which, in turn, support diverse bird species. Tallamy argues that incorporating native plants into gardens is a powerful conservation action. Dr Sara Oldfield, a leading expert in biodiversity conservation, highlights the importance of preserving native plant species for global biodiversity. In her work with the Botanic Gardens Conservation International (BGCI), a charity based in Kew, she emphasises the role of botanic gardens in safeguarding threatened plant species, including many that are crucial to local ecosystems:

> The preservation of native plant species is fundamental to maintaining the diversity of life on Earth. Native plants are the building blocks of ecosystems, supporting a wide range of wildlife and contributing to the ecological balance. Without them, we risk losing not just plants, but the entire web of life that depends on them.[††]

So, why do native and climate-adapted plants matter? Well, selecting native plants establishes ecological harmony by aligning gardens with the natural flora of the region. This not only preserves local biodiversity but also fosters a sense of place, connecting the garden to the broader ecosystem. Native plants provide habitats and essential food sources for wildlife and are inherently suited to the local climate, often requiring less water than exotic species, a particularly essential consideration in areas facing drought conditions and water scarcity. Gardens with a focus on these plants contribute to water conservation and sustainable landscaping practices.

Plants that have evolved in specific climates are better equipped to handle the extremes associated

---

[††] Sara Oldfield, *Great Botanic Gardens of the World*, New Holland Publishers, 2007.

with climate change. They have developed adaptive mechanisms that enhance their resilience, making them valuable assets in the creation of climate-resilient gardens. In this intricate balance between flora and climate, native plants emerge as resilient protagonists, equipped with adaptive mechanisms finely tuned by evolution. As climate change ushers in a new era of extremes – from scorching heatwaves to intense storms and erratic rainfall patterns – these plants showcase a remarkable ability to weather environmental challenges.

Native plants, defined as such by their historical presence in a specific region, have evolved in harmony with the climatic nuances of their surroundings. This co-evolutionary process has given them a suite of physical properties that enable them to navigate the challenges posed by climate change. These mechanisms, often subtle and intricate, reflect the plant kingdom's resilience honed over millennia. Native plants in arid or semi-arid regions have developed remarkable drought-tolerance mechanisms. Deep root systems enable them to tap into water reserves deep in the soil, while some species exhibit modified leaf structures to minimise water loss through transpiration. In regions prone to heatwaves, native plants employ various strategies to cope with elevated temperatures. Light-reflecting leaf surfaces, the ability to adjust metabolic processes and the synthesis of heat-shock proteins are among the mechanisms that help mitigate the impacts of extreme heat.

Coastal native plants face the challenge of braving intense storms and salt spray. To counter these adversities, certain species have evolved flexible stems that can bend with the wind, while others have developed structures to excrete salt, preventing its accumulation in sensitive tissues. In areas prone to erratic rainfall and flooding, native plants show-case adaptations to waterlogged conditions. Some species have specialised root structures that enhance oxygen uptake, while others exhibit a capacity for rapid growth following floods, allowing them to recover swiftly.

Biodiversity, the rich tapestry woven by diverse native plant species, lies at the heart of ecosys-tem resilience. The intricate web of relationships between plants, animals and micro-organisms forms a resilient fabric that can absorb and recover from disturbances, including those exacerbated by climate change. Different species have varied responses to environmental stressors, ensuring that if one species faces challenges, others may thrive, maintaining overall ecosystem function. Native plants' mutualistic bond with wildlife enhances the reproductive success of both plants and pollinators, ensuring the continued propagation of native flora even in the face of climate-induced disruptions.

Native plants contribute to soil health and carbon sequestration, bolstering ecosystem resilience. Their root systems enhance soil structure, preventing erosion during storms and sequestering carbon through the accumulation of organic matter, further mitigating the impacts of climate change. Recognising the intrinsic value of native plants in the context of climate change, conservation and restoration efforts plays a pivotal role in preserving and enhancing plant resilience. Strategic interventions, such as habitat protection, reforestation and the removal of invasive species help bolster the adaptive capacity of native plant populations.

Conservation efforts prioritise the preservation of genetic diversity within native plant populations. Restoration ecology seeks to recreate or rehabilitate ecosystems that have been degraded or altered – the loss of tropical rainforests to monoculture farming and the planting of new trees is a good example. Planting native species in degraded areas enhances ecosystem resilience by reintroducing key components of the original plant community. Invasive species can outcompete native plants and disrupt established ecosystems. Effective management strategies involve the removal or control of invasive species, allowing native flora to reclaim their ecological niches.

While native plants possess inherent resilience, the unprecedented pace and magnitude of contemporary climate change present formidable challenges. Anthropogenic factors, including habitat fragmentation, pollution and the global movement of species, compound the pressures on native flora. Urbanisation and land-use changes contribute to habitat fragmentation, isolating plant populations and hindering their ability to migrate in response to changing climates. Connectivity between natural areas becomes crucial for facilitating plant movement.

Climate change prompts shifts in the geographical ranges of plant species. While some may naturally migrate to suitable climates, others may face barriers such as human infrastructure or incompatible ecosystems. Conservation strategies must consider assisted migration to support plant adaptation. Climate change interacts with other environmental stressors, such as pollution, altering ecological dynamics. Native plants must contend with changing soil compositions, atmospheric conditions and new challenges that may influence their adaptive strategies.

Despite the clear benefits, challenges exist when it comes to promoting native and climate-adapted plants. Gardeners may face limitations in the availability of such plants in commercial nurseries. Additionally, the aesthetic appeal of exotic species may pose a challenge in shifting cultural preferences towards a more naturalistic, native-focused approach. Thankfully the internet and apps, both of them visual mechanisms, can help educate new and seasoned gardeners alike about the beauty of native and climate-adapted plants.

Several countries have recognised the significance of native plants in gardening and biodiversity conservation, leading to the implementation of policies and initiatives to promote their use. In the United States, for example, initiatives such as the National Wildlife Federation's *Native Plant Finder* provide resources for gardeners to identify and incorporate native plants into their landscapes. Similar initiatives exist in countries like the United Kingdom, Australia and Canada, showcasing a growing global awareness of the importance of native and climate-adapted plants in resilient gardening.

Water-Efficient Practices

In areas affected by climate change, water scarcity is a significant concern. Resilient gardens employ water-efficient landscaping practices, including the use of drip irrigation, rainwater harvesting and the selection of drought-tolerant plants. As mentioned above, mulching around plants helps retain soil moisture, reducing the need for frequent watering. Such water scarcity, and the unpredictable precipitation patterns due to climate change, necessitate a paradigm shift in gardening practices. Water-efficient landscaping emerges as a critical strategy, emphasising the conservation and responsible use of water resources. Therefore, gardens worldwide are adapting to a new era where sustainable water management is essential for resilience and longevity.

As well as the previously mentioned strategies being used in Israel, in response to prolonged droughts, southern California has embraced sustainable landscaping initiatives. The Metropolitan Water District of Southern California promotes water-efficient landscaping with a focus on native and drought-tolerant plants. Rebate programmes incentivise residents to replace water-intensive lawns with low-water-use alternatives, contributing to regional water conservation efforts. Incentive programmes offered by some local councils and municipalities further encourage homeowners to invest in water-efficient practices, demonstrating the economic benefits of sustainable gardening.

Dr Peter Gleick, a co-founder of the Pacific Institute and a leading expert on water and climate, emphasises the urgency of water-efficient practices in the face of climate change. He notes that 'water efficiency is the cheapest, fastest and most environmentally sensitive way to meet the growing demand for water'.[‡‡] Landscape designer Julie Moir Messervy writes about the aesthetic possibilities of water-efficient landscaping. She notes that well-designed, water-efficient gardens can be not only visually stunning but also environmentally responsible. She encourages a shift towards creating landscapes that harmonise with nature and use water judiciously.

Climate change exacerbates water scarcity in many regions, making efficient water use imperative. In regions facing acute water scarcity, such as parts of Australia, California and the Middle East, these

‡‡ Dr Peter Gleick, 'Water efficiency key to solving crisis', Xylem, Pacific Institute, 2014.

practices are crucial for sustainable gardening. It also needs to be remembered that excessive water use in landscaping can lead to the depletion of local water bodies and negatively impact ecosystems. Water-efficient gardening helps maintain the balance of local water systems, preventing over-extraction and protecting aquatic habitats. This is particularly relevant in regions with fragile ecosystems, such as wetlands and riparian areas (those related to or situated on the banks of a river, stream or other body of water).

As gardeners, we need to look towards practical water-saving measures. Water-efficient landscaping practices, such as using permeable surfaces, help retain soil moisture while reducing evaporation and suppressing weed growth. Permeable surfaces allow rainwater to infiltrate the soil, replenishing ground-water, preventing flooding and supporting healthy root systems. Many traditional irrigation systems are energy-intensive. Water-efficient technologies, such as rainwater harvesting, reduce the energy foot-print associated with water distribution.

Water-efficient landscaping is not just a response to the immediate challenges of climate change; it's a forward-looking strategy for sustainable gardening – a 'true' look at the 'future of gardening'. As water becomes an increasingly precious resource, the adoption of practices that promote responsible water use is not only environmentally responsible but also economically sensible.

Soil Health

Healthy soils contribute to the overall resilience of a garden. Resilient gardening practices focus on building soil structure, improving fertility through adding organic matter and minimising soil disturbance. Healthy soils better retain water, support plant growth and provide a buffer against extreme weather events. As global temperatures fluctuate, weather patterns become more unpredictable and extreme events become more frequent, building and maintaining healthy soils is essential for gardeners worldwide. From organic practices to regenerative agriculture, the focus on soil health is not only about fostering robust plant growth but also about mitigating climate-related challenges and contributing to broader environmental conservation.

Dr Elaine Ingham, a prominent soil microbiologist, advocates for a focus on the 'soil food web' – the complex interactions between soil micro-organisms and plants. She emphasises that healthy soils are teeming with life, including bacteria, fungi, protozoa and nematodes, all of which play crucial roles in nutrient cycling and plant health.

Gardeners know that healthy soils provide essential nutrients for plant growth. Micro-organisms in the soil break down organic matter, releasing nutrients in forms that plants can absorb. Soil health is directly linked to the availability of vital elements like nitrogen, phosphorus and potassium, influencing plant nutrition and overall garden productivity. Well-structured soils with good organic content have improved water retention and drainage properties. This is crucial for gardens facing the challenges of climate change, including both drought and heavy rainfall. Healthy soils act like sponges, holding water during dry periods and preventing waterlogging during intense rainfall.

Healthy soils help mitigate the impacts of climate change via carbon sequestration, the process by which carbon dioxide (CO_2) is captured from the atmosphere and stored for long periods in natural or artificial reservoirs. This not only improves soil structure and fertility but also contributes to the reduction of atmospheric carbon dioxide levels. Soil erosion is a global challenge exacerbated by climate-related events such as intense rainfall, flooding, flash flooding and storms. As mentioned earlier, healthy soils with robust root systems and organic matter are more resistant to erosion. Cover crops, contour ploughing (the agricultural practice of ploughing, planting and other farming activities that are conducted along the natural contours of the land, rather than in straight lines up and down slopes) and the maintenance of ground cover contribute to erosion control, preserving the integrity of the topsoil.

Regenerative agriculture, with its emphasis on improving soil health and biodiversity, has gained traction in the United States. Farmers and gardeners adopting regenerative practices focus on minimal soil disturbance, cover cropping and rotational grazing. The Rodale Institute's Farming Systems Trial, a long-term study of regenerative agriculture launched in 1981, has shown positive outcomes in terms of soil health, carbon sequestration and crop yields. In fact, organic matter has increased with larger microbial biomass, diversity and activity while reducing soil compaction. Organic management increases water infiltration and doesn't contribute to the accumulation of toxins in waterways. Further studies like Rodale need to be undertaken around the world to ensure that gardening in the future adopts a connected approach, with humankind as the leaders and smart technology, AI and vigorous research assisting for the betterment of all.

In response to soil degradation and environmental concerns, China has implemented agroecological practices. These practices, which include organic farming, agroforestry and cover cropping, aim to restore and maintain soil health. China's experience highlights the global recognition of the importance of sustainable soil management for food security and environmental sustainability.

Dr Rattan Lal, a leading soil scientist and recipient of the Nobel Prize, emphasises the role of healthy soils in climate mitigation. He notes that 'soil is the only option we have to sequester carbon dioxide at a scale that can make a difference'.[§§] Lal highlights that improving soil health is not only vital for sustainable agriculture but also for addressing the broader challenges of climate change.

A thriving soil ecosystem is rich in biodiversity that supports plant health, enhances natural pest control and contributes to the overall resilience of the garden's ecosystem. Healthy soils create a

§§ Hunter Lovins, 'Regenerative agriculture: Key to solving the climate crisis', Climate & Capital Media, 2023.

balanced environment where plants can coexist with a diverse community of organisms.

Holistic grazing, a regenerative practice, has gained popularity in Australia. By mimicking natural grazing patterns and allowing for periods of rest, this practice enhances soil health and promotes the growth of diverse plant species. Improved soil health, in turn, supports the resilience of pasture ecosystems, contributing to sustainable agriculture. In Brazil, agroforestry systems integrate trees and crops, fostering a symbiotic relationship between agriculture and forestry. These systems contribute to soil health by enhancing nutrient cycling, improving water retention and reducing soil erosion. The Amazon region has seen initiatives promoting agroforestry as a sustainable alternative to traditional land use.

Internationally, organisations like the Food and Agriculture Organization (FAO) of the United Nations promote sustainable soil management. The Global Soil Partnership, initiated by the FAO, emphasises the importance of soil health for achieving food security and environmental sustainability. A worldwide implementation of soil health practices, however, could be challenging on many levels, not least the need for education and awareness among gardeners, the initial costs associated with transitioning to organic or regenerative methods and the time required for soil restoration. Additionally, urban gardens may face constraints related to limited space and potential soil contamination.

The centrality of soil health in creating resilient gardens is nevertheless evident in the interconnected web of ecological processes that occur beneath our feet. As gardeners and agricultural practitioners embrace regenerative and sustainable soil management practices, they not only enhance the productivity of their immediate surroundings but also contribute to global efforts in climate mitigation and environmental conservation. Soil health stands as the foundation upon which sustainable and resilient gardens are built, offering a path towards a more harmonious relationship between human cultivation and the natural world.

The Adaptable Gardener
Resilient gardening also involves adapting traditional practices based on climate patterns. Resilient gardeners actively monitor local climate trends on the internet or on apps on their phones and adjust their gardening strategies accordingly. From adjusting planting calendars to preparing for unexpected

weather conditions and experimenting with new plant varieties, adaptive gardening is not only about responding to current climate conditions but also about building resilience for an uncertain future.

In the Netherlands, and elsewhere in the world where climate change affects precipitation patterns, gardeners are implementing climate-responsive practices. Rain gardens, designed to capture and manage excess rainwater, help prevent flooding during intense rainfall events. Additionally, the selection of plant varieties that can withstand both drought and heavy rain contributes to the adaptability of Dutch gardens.

Dr Kim E. Dooley, a horticulturist with expertise in sustainable gardening, notes that: 'adaptive gardening is about being observant and willing to make changes based on what the environment is telling you. It's a dynamic process that requires a deep understanding of the local climate and ecosystems.'¶¶ The late Beth Chatto, a renowned plantswoman and writer, known for her expertise in ecological

---

¶¶ Phuong Bach Huynh, Theresa Pesl Murphrey, Kim E. Dooley, Robert Strong and Larry M. Dooley, 'An examination of postsecondary agricultural education instructors' perspectives of the case study instructional technique and the development of a model to encourage use', *Journal of Agricultural Education*, 60(3), 2019, pp. 173–190.

gardening, believed in the power of observing nature for inspiration. She stated: 'Right plant, right place – it's so simple yet so often ignored. One of the most adaptable 'plants' in a garden is the gardener.'***

Gardeners need to be attuned to changes in temperature, precipitation and growing seasons. This is where the internet, and particularly phone apps, is indispensable. These will grow technologically and in popularity and become more efficient as the years pass. In regions experiencing earlier springs or delayed frosts, adapting the planting schedule ensures that plants are introduced at the optimal time for successful growth. As climate conditions shift, certain plant varieties may become less suitable for traditional gardening. Adaptive gardeners experiment with new plant varieties that are better suited to the changing climate. These may include heat-tolerant plants for hotter summers or varieties resistant to specific pests and diseases.

Gardens often contain microclimates – small, localised areas with unique temperature, humidity and light conditions. Adaptive gardening involves recognising and managing these microclimates

***Beth Chatto, *The Beth Chatto Garden Notebook*, Orion, 1988.

to create optimal conditions for specific plants. For example, plants can be positioned near walls for added warmth or for providing shade during heatwaves or shelter from extreme wind patterns. Strategic placement of shade structures, windbreaks and companion planting can create microenvironments that protect plants from extreme weather conditions, fostering their resilience.

As mentioned earlier, water scarcity is a concern in many regions affected by climate change. Therefore, it comes as no surprise that adaptive gardeners employ water-conserving practices such as mulching, drip irrigation and rainwater harvesting. These strategies help ensure efficient water use, especially during periods of drought, while also mitigating soil erosion and promoting soil health.

Changing climate conditions can influence the prevalence of pests and diseases, so adaptive gardeners implement Integrated Pest Management (IPM) strategies, which prioritise preventive measures and natural controls over chemical interventions. This approach ensures a more organic, sustainable and environmentally friendly approach to pest and disease management.

Community gardens in Canada are implementing adaptive practices to address the challenges of a changing climate. Workshops and educational programmes help gardeners understand the impact of climate change on local ecosystems. These initiatives encourage the adoption of adaptive strategies, such as choosing heat-tolerant plant varieties and incorporating water-saving technologies. And allotment gardens in the UK, where gardeners cultivate small plots of land, are adapting to shifting climate patterns. Gardeners are experimenting with crops that were traditionally grown in warmer climates, adjusting planting dates and exploring water-efficient irrigation methods. This adaptive approach ensures the continued productivity of allotment gardens despite changing conditions. Internationally, organisations such as the Royal Horticultural Society (RHS) in the UK and the American Horticultural Society (AHS) provide resources and guidance on adaptive gardening. These organisations recognise how important it is to support gardeners in navigating the challenges of climate change and encourage the adoption of adaptive practices.

Permaculture

Permaculture, with its emphasis on sustainable and regenerative design, aligns well with resilient gardening practices. By incorporating permaculture principles such as polyculture (the agricultural practice in which multiple different crops or plant species are grown together in the same area simultaneously, rather than cultivating a single crop (as in monoculture), companion planting and IPM, gardens become more self-sustaining and resilient to external challenges.For example, companion planting, such as marigolds by the side of vegetables, can help deter nematodes and other pests or attract beneficial insects near susceptible crops. Rooted in designing systems that mimic natural ecosystems, permaculture stands as a guiding philosophy for creating resilient gardens in the face of climate change. Embracing principles that prioritise sustainability, biodiversity and regenerative practices, permaculture offers a holistic approach to gardening that mitigates climate change's impacts and actively contributes to ecological health.

Careful observation of the natural world and the local environment are key when starting permaculture practices. Gardeners assess factors such as sunlight, wind patterns and water flow. This deep understanding allows for informed interaction with the landscape, optimising the use of resources and minimising environmental impact. In addition, permaculture encourages the harvesting and storage of energy in various forms, such as sunlight, water and organic matter. This principle involves capturing and utilising available resources efficiently. Examples include rainwater harvesting, the use of solar energy systems and the adoption of composting to store nutrients for plants.

Gardens designed on permaculture principles aim to provide tangible benefits. Whether through food production, the growing of medicinal plants or habitat creation, obtaining a yield ensures that the garden serves practical purposes while supporting ecosystem health. Permaculture systems are designed to be self-regulating, minimising external inputs. This principle involves observing and adapting to feedback from the environment. For instance, if a plant is struggling, gardeners will be prompted to analyse and address any underlying issues rather than resorting to chemical intervention.

In permaculture, the use of renewable resources and ecosystem services are paramount. This involves incorporating plants and practices that harness natural processes, such as nitrogen-fixing plants, which enhance soil fertility, or companion plant-ing to encourage beneficial insect populations. The concept of *waste* is reimagined in permaculture as a valuable resource. Gardeners strive to minimise waste by reusing and recycling materials, implementing composting systems and creating closed-loop cycles within the garden.

Permaculture designs are informed by patterns found in nature. This approach involves the recognition of larger ecological patterns and their application to specific garden designs. For example, understanding natural water flow patterns can inform the placement of swales (shallow, vegetated channels or ditches designed to manage water runoff, slow down its flow, and promote its infiltration into the soil) and water catchment systems. Permaculture also encourages the integration of diverse elements within a garden ecosystem. This can include incorporating plants that support each other or designing polyculture systems that mimic natural ecosystems and enhance resilience.

Permaculture favours gradual, small-scale solutions over large, rapid interventions. This principle acknowledges the complexity of ecosystems and promotes thoughtful, incremental changes that allow for adaptation and learning. Biodiversity is a cornerstone of permaculture design. Diverse plantings create resilient ecosystems that are better equipped to withstand pests, diseases and changing environmental conditions – an interconnectedness and interdependence of species within a garden.

Zaytuna Farm, Australia, established by permaculture co-founder Geoff Lawton, serves as a prominent example of permaculture principles in action. The farm incorporates swales for water management, agroforestry practices and diverse plantings to create a self-sustaining and regenerative system. Meanwhile, Martin Crawford's Forest Garden in the UK exemplifies permaculture principles by emulating the structure and function of a natural forest. The garden integrates fruit and nut trees, shrubs and perennial plants in layered configurations, maximising productivity while minimising the need for external inputs. Geoff Lawton emphasises the potential of permaculture to address environmental challenges, stating: 'All the world's problems can be solved in a garden.'[†††] He advocates for the regenerative capacity of permaculture to restore ecosystems and create sustainable, productive landscapes. The late Dr Toby Hemenway, another influential permaculturist and author, stressed the importance of designing gardens that

---

††† Linda Buzzell, Geoff Lawton, 'All the World's Problems Can Be Solved in a Garden', *Permaculture News*, 2008.

mimic natural systems. He stated: 'Permaculture is about designing human systems that are more like natural systems.'‡‡‡

Permaculture places a strong emphasis on building and maintaining healthy soil through practices such as mulching, composting and minimal soil disturbance. Healthy soils contribute to water retention, nutrient cycling and the overall vitality of the garden. As in resilient gardening, the diversity of plant species in permaculture designs allows for a range of climate-adapted plants to be incorporated. This approach ensures that the garden can thrive under varying climate conditions, from heatwaves to heavy rainfall. By prioritising biodiversity and mimicking natural ecosystems, permaculture gardens can support beneficial insects, pollinators and natural predators, contributing to a balanced and healthy garden ecology.

Permaculture also promotes localised food production, reducing the carbon footprint associated with food transportation. Gardens designed using permaculture principles can contribute to local food resilience by providing fresh produce and supporting community food systems. This, too,

---

‡‡‡ Toby Hemenway, *The Permaculture City*, Chelsea Green Publishing, 2015.

aims to minimise waste by creating a closed loop. Permaculture is not just a set of practices but a philosophy that encourages community engagement and education. Through workshops, permaculture designs and community gardens, this approach fosters a deeper understanding of ecological principles and promotes sustainable living. It's primarily a grassroots movement, and its principles are applied by individuals and communities worldwide. While there are no specific global policies dedicated to permaculture, the principles align with broader sustainability goals, and some local initiatives may support permaculture practices.

Certainly, permaculture principles provide a road map for designing gardens – a factor which has been invaluable to me as a garden designer – that are not only resilient to the challenges of a changing climate but actively contribute to ecological health.

Climate-Smart Garden Design

In the face of a changing climate, the design of resilient gardens becomes an imperative. A climate-smart approach to garden design involves thoughtful consideration of various environmental factors to create landscapes that can not only endure but thrive in the midst of evolving climatic conditions. By understanding wind patterns, harnessing microclimates and embracing seasonal variations, gardeners can craft environments that foster plant health, conserve water and contribute to overall ecological resilience.

Wind can be a formidable force, adversely affecting plant growth, soil moisture and overall garden health. Integrating windbreaks into garden design is a climate-smart strategy to mitigate the negative effects of strong winds. Windbreaks are typically composed of trees, shrubs or other structures strategically placed to reduce wind speed and create a sheltered microenvironment. Careful consideration of the prevailing wind direction is crucial for effective windbreak design. Planting windbreaks on the windward side of the garden helps create a buffer zone, protecting delicate plants from the full force of strong winds.

Additionally, windbreaks can be strategically positioned to channel airflow away from sensitive areas. Choosing the right plants to use as windbreaks is essential. Deciduous trees that lose their leaves in winter can provide protection during the summer months while allowing sunlight to penetrate in the winter. Evergreen trees and shrubs offer year-round protection. Combining different species

can enhance the diversity and resilience of the windbreak. The height and density of the windbreak
influence its effectiveness. Taller trees and shrubs
can create a more substantial barrier against strong
winds, while layering different plant heights within
the windbreak design contributes to a more efficient
reduction in wind speed at various levels.

In Mali, West Africa, agroforestry systems
integrate windbreaks to protect crops from desert
winds. Acacia and eucalyptus trees are strategically
planted to reduce wind erosion and create a more
favourable microclimate for agricultural activities.
Orchards in New Zealand often incorporate windbreaks to shield fruit trees from strong prevailing
winds. Rows of densely planted trees provide
protection, reducing the risk of wind damage to
blossoms, young fruit and branches.

As temperatures rise due to climate change, providing shade becomes a critical aspect of garden
design. Shade structures offer relief to plants sensitive
to excessive heat and help conserve soil moisture.
Additionally, shaded areas create comfortable spaces
for gardeners and visitors to enjoy the outdoors.
Identifying areas that receive intense sunlight and
strategically placing shade structures can help create
cool zones within the garden. This is particularly

important for plants that prefer partial or dappled shade. Deploying adaptable shade structures allows for seasonal adjustments. Retractable or moveable shade structures enable gardeners to modulate sunlight exposure based on changing weather patterns and plants' requirements. The choice of materials for shade structures influences their effectiveness. Materials with reflective properties can help bounce sunlight away, reducing heat absorption. Additionally, materials with good ventilation allow for air circulation, preventing heat build-up. Perhaps the first option for shade, however, is a tree. Not only is it a natural addition, but it adds to the biodiversity of the garden, attracts wildlife, reduces wind and creates a shady spot, perfect for shade-loving plants.

Japanese gardens often feature intricate shade structures known as *kakehi* or *kakejiku*. These structures, made of bamboo and fabric, are strategically placed to provide shade to delicate moss gardens, maintaining a cool and tranquil environment. Singapore's botanical gardens use modern shade structures to protect sensitive plant collections from the tropical sun. These structures, often made of lightweight materials, create shaded areas where temperature and humidity are carefully regulated.

Water is a precious resource, and incorporating water features into a garden design contributes to both aesthetic appeal and climate resilience. Climate-smart gardens utilise water features strategically to enhance moisture retention, provide habitat for wildlife and create microclimates that support plant health. Integrating rainwater harvesting systems into garden design allows for the collection and storage of rainfall. Rain barrels, cisterns or permeable surfaces that direct water to plant beds contribute to more sustainable water use. Water features, such as ponds or fountains, can influence the microclimate of a garden. Evaporation from water surfaces can cool the surrounding air, creating a more favourable environment for plants and reducing the overall temperature. Water features attract wildlife, contributing to biodiversity in the garden. Birds, insects and amphibians are drawn to water sources, creating a balanced ecosystem where natural predators help control pests.

The historic Alhambra Gardens in Spain, as seen in *Royal Gardens of the World*, showcase the use of intricate water features, including fountains, pools and irrigation channels. These features not only add to the aesthetic beauty of the gardens but also contribute to microclimate regulation in the arid climate of Andalusia. In Indonesia, Balinese gardens often incorporate water features such as ponds and flowing water channels. These features not only serve as reflective and calming elements but also contribute to temperature moderation in the tropical climate. Jinny Blom, a landscape designer, emphasises the importance of thoughtful garden design in adapting to the changing climate: 'Garden design has a huge role to play in mitigating climate change. By planting trees and creating water features, we can make a real difference in microclimates.'§§§

Dr Katharine Hayhoe, a climate scientist, highlights the interconnectedness of climate-smart design with broader environmental goals. She notes: 'The more we can align solutions for a stable climate with solutions for clean air and water, and for people's well-being, the more we'll be able to achieve multiple goals with single actions.'¶¶¶

While climate-smart garden design offers numerous benefits, challenges may include the need for continuous monitoring, the adaptation of designs to evolving

§§§ Jinny Blom, *What Makes a Garden: a considered approach to garden design*, Frances Lincoln, 2023.
¶¶¶ Katharine Hayhoe, 'Climate Solutions: Lots of Silver Buckshot', Polar Bears & the Changing Arctic, 2020; or at https://polarbearsinternational.org/news-media/articles/climate-solutions-scientist-katharine-hayhoe.

climate patterns, and the necessity of considering the long-term viability of plant selections. Additionally, the integration of sustainable practices, such as rainwater harvesting, may require initial investment and infrastructure. Climate-smart gardening aligns with broader initiatives promoting sustainable and resilient landscapes. Some regions have implemented policies that encourage water conservation, green infrastructure and climate-resilient urban planning. International organisations, including the United Nations Framework Convention on Climate Change (UNFCCC), now recognise the role of green spaces in climate adaptation.

Climate-smart garden design represents a proactive and adaptive approach to cultivating resilient landscapes. By integrating windbreaks, shade structures and water features, gardeners can address the challenges posed by climate change while creating beautiful and functional outdoor spaces. Climate-smart principles not only endure the impacts of a changing climate but actively contribute to the conservation of natural resources and biodiversity. As gardens become microcosms of sustainable living, the practice of climate-smart design becomes an essential tool for nurturing both plant life and the health of our planet.

Wildlife-Friendly Gardening

Gardens that support local wildlife contribute to ecological resilience. Planting flowers rich in nectar, providing habitat features like bird houses and insect hotels and avoiding the use of harmful pesticides help create a balanced ecosystem. Biodiversity in the garden enhances its ability to adapt to changing conditions. Wildlife-friendly gardening goes beyond mere aesthetics; it's a conscientious effort to create spaces that support local flora and fauna, contributing to ecological resilience in the face of environmental challenges. Gardeners can therefore craft environments that harmonise with the broader ecosystem. Wildlife-friendly gardening enhances biodiversity, fosters ecological resilience and becomes a cornerstone for sustainable horticultural practices.

One of the fundamental pillars of wildlife-friendly gardening is the cultivation of nectar-rich flowers. These blooms serve as vital food sources for pollinators such as bees, butterflies and birds. The symbiotic relationship between flowering plants and pollinators contributes to the reproduction of many plant species and supports the entire ecosystem. A diverse array of flowering plants ensures a continuous supply of nectar throughout the growing season. Selecting plants with different bloom times and flower shapes accommodates the varied preferences of pollinators. As mentioned earlier, native plants are well adapted to local eco-systems and often have intricate relationships with native pollinators. Incorporating native species in garden design enhances the ecological relevance and resilience of the garden. Hybridised plants may lack the nectar or pollen content necessary for the sustenance of pollinators; therefore, choosing heirloom or non-hybridised varieties ensures that plants retain their natural characteristics, providing valuable resources for wildlife. Of course, there is something to be said for leaving lawns to grow a little longer so beneficial insects and pollinators can enjoy native dandelion or clover flowers. The idea of *rewilding* a garden, allowing native plants to settle in your garden and leaving areas a little messy, helps towards biodiversity and sustainability in the garden setting, which, in turn, can have a positive impact on the larger environment.

Costa Rica is renowned for its butterfly gar-dens, where a complex tapestry of nectar-rich plants attracts an astonishing diversity of butterfly species. Native flowering plants, such as lantana and verbena, play a vital role in sustaining these delicate pollinators. And the United Kingdom has seen a resurgence of wildflower meadows as part of wildlife-friendly, naturalistic gardening initiatives. Meadows filled with native wildflowers like ox-eye daisies and red clover provide abundant nectar sources for bees and butterflies.

Beyond providing food sources, wildlife-friendly gardening involves incorporating habitat features that offer shelter, nesting sites and refuge for various species. Bird houses, insect hotels and brush piles create diverse micro-habitats that support a wide range of wildlife. Placing habitat features in different areas of the garden ensures that wildlife has access to various microclimates and environments. Bird houses in sheltered spots and insect hotels in sunny locations cater to the specific needs of different species. Using natural, locally sourced and recycled materials in the construction of habitat features enhances their appeal to wildlife. Different species may have specific requirements; for instance, bee hotels with varying-sized cavities cater to different bee species. Wildlife needs shelter and nesting sites throughout the year. Planning for year-round habitat provision, such as leaving some areas of the garden undisturbed during winter, ensures a continuous haven for creatures large and small.

Bat boxes are strategically placed in gardens across the United States to provide roosting sites for these nocturnal insectivores. Bats play a crucial role in pest control, making them valuable allies in wildlife-friendly gardening. In the UK, efforts to create hedgehog-friendly gardens involve incorporating hedgehog houses and leaving access points in fences to create the hedgehog highway. These features help hedgehogs find safe spaces for nesting and hibernating.

The use of harmful pesticides poses a significant threat to wildlife, especially to beneficial insects and pollinators. Wildlife-friendly gardening emphasises organic, natural pest control methods and promotes the cultivation of a balanced ecosystem where predators and prey coexist harmoniously. Encouraging natural predators, such as ladybirds, spiders and predatory beetles, helps control pest populations without resorting to chemical intervention. Planting flowers that attract these predators creates a healthier and more resilient garden. Wildlife-friendly gardeners often adopt a more tolerant approach to minor pest issues, recognising that a few pests are a natural part of a diverse ecosystem that help maintain a balance where predators can control pest populations. Italy has seen a surge in organic farming practices, where farmers prioritise natural methods of pest control. These practices contribute to healthier soils, increased biodiversity and reduced environmental impact. Many community gardens in Canada, for example, follow pesticide-free principles, emphasising sustainable and organic gardening methods. These gardens not only produce healthy, locally grown food but also support urban biodiversity.

The fundamental essence of wildlife-friendly gardening lies in its ability to enhance biodiversity. A garden teeming with a variety of plants, insects, birds and other wildlife forms a resilient and adaptable ecosystem. Biodiversity contributes to the stability and sustainability of the garden, allowing it to withstand environmental fluctuations and challenges. Diverse ecosystems provide essential services, such as pollination, soil fertility and natural pest control. Biodiversity in the garden ensures the continued provision of these services, supporting plant health and productivity. The presence of a range of plant species, each with its unique set of adaptations, enhances the overall resilience of the garden. Wildlife-friendly gardening therefore contributes directly to wildlife conservation by providing habitat and food sources for diverse species. This is particularly important in urban areas where natural habitats may be scarce.

Gardens rich in biodiversity also offer educational opportunities for individuals and communities. Observing the interactions between different species fosters a deeper understanding of ecological processes and the interconnectedness of all living things. Several international initiatives and organisations promote wildlife-friendly gardening and biodiversity conservation. The United Nations Decade on Ecosystem Restoration, for example, encourages global efforts to restore ecosystems, including gardens, in order to enhance biodiversity and ecological resilience. Wildlife-friendly gardening is a powerful and accessible tool enabling individuals to contribute to biodiversity conservation and ecological resilience. Gardeners become stewards of vibrant and thriving ecosystems. Wildlife-friendly gardening creates not only beautiful and sustainable gardens but also interconnected landscapes that play a crucial role for our planet. As we cultivate harmony with nature in our own patches of green, we actively participate in the global effort to foster biodiversity, protect wildlife and build resilient ecosystems for generations to come.

Continuous Learning and Adaptation

Resilient gardeners embrace a mindset of continuous learning and adaptation. Staying informed about climate trends, experimenting with new techniques and being open to adjusting gardening practices based on experience contribute to the garden's ability to thrive despite particular uncertainties. This has certainly been my approach to gardening.

Regular monitoring of climate data, via online platforms, local weather stations and climate prediction models, can be a valuable resource. Observing local changes in flora and fauna, such as the timing of flowering plants or the arrival of migratory birds, can offer anecdotal evidence of shifts in the local climate. This knowledge can inform planting schedules and species selection.

Engaging with gardening communities, local horticultural societies and environmental organisations provides opportunities to share observations, exchange knowledge and collectively respond to climate challenges. With the internet, email and instantaneous messaging (IM), knowledge can be shared in an instant. Who knows where this will go in the future? Perhaps we shall have implants that we can trigger with our thoughts, bring up ideas, share knowledge and participate in online community group chats through the lenses in our eyes.

Collaboration fosters a collective intelligence that benefits individual gardeners and the broader community. If AI taps into this collective intelligence then the benefits could be far-reaching and international. Perhaps AI will be able to predict and even alter weather patterns, and, with the use of AI-connected robots, specific plants that can cope with extreme weather patterns will be automatically planted. AI and resilient gardeners will embrace the role of the scientist in their outdoor laboratories, continuously experimenting with new techniques to optimise plant health, soil fertility and overall garden productivity.

In addition, experimentation involves a willingness to try new methods and techniques, recognising that some may succeed while others may not – this is how I learnt to garden. This trial-and-error approach allows gardeners to refine their practices based on first-hand experience. Experimenting with sustainable gardening practices, such as permaculture, companion planting and organic gardening, contributes to ecological resilience. Resilient gardeners will need to explore and adopt innovative technologies that align with sustainable gardening. Experimenting with different soil amendments, cover cropping and composting techniques will allow gardeners to tailor soil conditions to the specific needs of their plants. Remember, healthy soil is the foundation of a resilient garden!

Continuous experimentation with pest and disease management methods helps gardeners identify effective, low-impact solutions. This may involve the use of biopesticides, companion planting for pest control or the fostering of natural predator–prey relationships.

Flexibility is a hallmark of resilient gardeners who remain open to adjusting their gardening practices based on experience, lessons learned and the evolving needs of the garden. Cultivating observational awareness allows gardeners to notice changes in plant health, the behaviour of wildlife and overall garden dynamics. This attentiveness provides early indicators that can inform adaptive actions. Reflecting on past gardening seasons, successes and challenges enables gardeners to refine their approaches.

I urge all gardeners, new and seasoned, to keep a written and photographic diary of their garden. This is essential for planning what to grow in future, where to grow something and observing how climate affects your day-to-day gardening practices. This introspective process allows for the identification of patterns and the continuous improvement of gardening practices. Your diary can also include monthly jobs pertinent to you, tips and tricks for getting the best out of your plants and garden, and sketches of garden design ideas.

Such a diary doesn't have to be a paper one. Online diaries and AI assistants are getting better at making life easier for you. With the possibility of attaching photographs and drawings you can create a full planner. Perhaps in the future gardeners will see that something is missing from their garden, or perhaps find that they need a specific tool to do a specific task, and a 3D printer will be able to print and create exactly what they require. 3D printers have already come down in price and their future possibilities are endless.

Engaging with the gardening community, attending workshops, online social events and participating in educational events is a great way to foster a culture of shared learning. Insights from fellow gardeners, professionals and experts contribute to a collective knowledge base that informs adaptive practices. Before the internet, email and IM, shared learning had to be done in person and at a particular place and time – often entailing miles of travel. With video conferencing, especially since the pandemic, all we have to do is fall out of bed in our pyjamas, log on, watch and listen. Online teaching is so easy now. Blogs, videos and podcasts have changed the way gardeners tap into information and how they want to be entertained. I never understood podcasts until I started listening to them while gardening. The content is invariably gardening related, but with interviews and gardening knowledge from experts in the field, I soon became a follower of specific podcasts. I also find it encouraging that now and, in the future, there will be a huge focus on Gen Z, who are looking for quality over quantity, especially with regard to sustainability. Being the first generation to be raised in an entirely digital world they will look towards gardening social media, podcasts and blogs, especially those that are updated regularly.

But that's not all. Observations of plant growth patterns, light exposure and water requirements may lead to adjustments in plant arrangements (this is where the gardener's diary comes in handy). Moving plants to more suitable locations within the garden optimises their chances of thriving. Reflecting on the performance of irrigation systems and watering schedules allows gardeners to fine-tune their approach. When faced with new pest or disease challenges, resilient gardeners adjust their pest management strategies. This may involve introducing natural predators, using targeted treatments or implementing preventive measures. The dynamic and adaptive nature of continuous learning enhances the ecological resilience of gardens. As gardeners respond to changing conditions, they create environments that can withstand climatic uncertainties and support diverse ecosystems. Experimenting with resource-efficient practices and technologies optimises resource use, minimising waste and environmental impact.

Resilient gardeners who embrace continuous learning often become ambassadors for sustainable gardening within their communities. Sharing knowledge, resources and experiences within gardening communities creates a support network. Community gardens, local gardening clubs and shared spaces foster collective resilience, allowing for a broader response to climate challenges. Community collaboration in gardening embodies a spirit of unity and shared purpose. It goes beyond the individual plot, reaching into the neighbourhood and the larger environment, into cities and even across continents. At its core, it's about people coming together, pooling their knowledge and combining their efforts to create vibrant, sustainable and resilient green spaces. In a community of gardeners, knowledge is a currency that flows freely. Experienced hands share insights with novices, passing down traditional wisdom alongside modern techniques. This collaborative exchange fosters a culture of continuous learning and growth. This is true of my grandparents who shared their knowledge and experience with me, while I, subsequently, shared my knowledge with millions via TV and the written word and, closer to home, with my nieces and great-nieces.

Community gardens often also become repositories of shared resources. From seeds and tools to compost and water, the collective pool of resources ensures that all members have access to the essentials for successful gardening. This not only reduces individual costs but also promotes sustainable practices. Gardening communities create a living classroom where experiences become valuable lessons. Successes and failures are shared openly, providing a rich tapestry of experiential learning. This communal knowledge bank becomes a source of resilience as gardeners collectively adapt to evolving challenges. These spaces not only produce fruits and vegetables but also cultivate a sense of belonging, shared responsibility and environmental stewardship.

Originating in Todmorden, United Kingdom, the 'Incredible Edible' movement encourages community gardening on public and unused land. Residents plant herbs and vegetables in accessible spaces, transforming the town into an edible landscape. This initiative exemplifies how a community's shared effort can redefine urban spaces and foster a sense of community resilience.

While continuous learning brings immense benefits, challenges may include information overload, the need for discernment in selecting relevant knowledge and the time and effort required for ongoing education. Overcoming these challenges requires a balance between curiosity and practical implementation.

Seed and plant swaps within gardening clubs promote biodiversity and enable members to diversify their gardens. Rare or locally adapted plant varieties are exchanged, contributing to the preservation of genetic diversity. It warms my heart to think that this activity of sharing plants will continue into the future; no matter how advanced technology gets, people, gardeners will still want this one-on-one interaction. Of course, gardening clubs often undertake community projects, such as beautifying public spaces, creating pollinator-friendly gardens or supporting local environmental initiatives. These projects showcase the impact that collective action can have on the broader community, and with 70 per cent of the world's population likely to live in urban environments by 2050, these community projects and shared spaces will be the breathing lungs of many cities.

Shared spaces, such as public parks or communal green areas within residential developments, become canvases for collective gardening efforts. These spaces foster a sense of shared ownership, encouraging residents to collaborate in transforming common areas into thriving green landscapes. Residents collaborating on the design and planning of shared spaces ensure that these areas reflect the diverse requirements and needs of the community. This participatory approach fosters a sense of pride and connection among residents. Designing shared spaces with accessibility in mind ensures that gardening activities are inclusive and welcoming to individuals of all ages and abilities. This inclusivity promotes a sense of belonging and shared responsibility for the well-being of the community.

In response to economic challenges and a shortage of imported goods, Cuba embraced urban agriculture as a means of self-sufficiency. Community gardens and cooperative farming initiatives sprouted across cities, showcasing the resilience that can emerge from shared efforts in gardening. Singapore's Housing and Development Board (HDB) estates incorporate community gardens, where residents can rent plots to cultivate their own crops. These shared spaces contribute to food security, foster community bonding and showcase the integration of gardening into urban planning. German cities have embraced the concept of urban greening, including communal gardening spaces within residential areas. These green pockets create opportunities for residents to connect with nature, collaborate on gardening projects and enhance the overall quality of urban living.

Community collaboration in gardening instils a sense of environmental stewardship. When individuals come together to care for shared green spaces, a collective responsibility for the health of the environment emerges. This shared stewardship extends beyond individual actions to benefit the broader ecosystem. Beyond the tangible benefits of shared resources and knowledge, community collaboration builds social resilience. The connections forged in gardening communities create networks of support that extend beyond horticulture, contributing to the overall well-being of individuals and the community. This informal and inclusive learning environment fosters a culture of continuous growth. And international initiatives recognise the significance of community collaboration in resilient gardening: the United Nations Sustainable Development Goals (SDGs), particularly Goal 11 (Sustainable Cities and Communities) and Goal 15 (Life on Land), highlight the importance of creating green spaces, fostering community engagement and promoting biodiversity within urban areas.

› › › › › ›

In summary, resilient gardening in the context of climate change involves a holistic and adaptive approach. By incorporating diverse plants, prioritising soil health, embracing water-efficient practices and fostering community collaboration, gardeners can contribute to the creation of gardens that not only withstand the challenges posed by climate change but also thrive in a changing environment.

In the future, as our climate changes and resources become scarcer, gardeners will need to stay informed and work together if there is to be any chance of success. None of us has a crystal ball, but the actions that we take now, as a collective, will affect the future of gardening.

Land Scarcity, Vertical Gardening, Augmented Reality and More

Land scarcity in urban environments is a pressing concern with far-reaching implications for future generations. As we grapple with the challenges of limited space, innovative solutions such as vertical gardening and farming have gained prominence, offering a glimpse into a more sustainable and space-efficient future. According to a report by the United Nations, over 50 per cent of the global population currently resides in urban areas, a figure which is projected to rise to c. 70 per cent by 2050.**** As cities expand to accommodate this influx, the demand for land intensifies, leading to increased

---

**** United Nations, Sustainable Development Goal 11, Sustainable Cities and Communities, 'Make cities and human settlements inclusive, safe, resilient and sustainable', 2022.

competition for space not only for housing but also for crucial green areas.

Vertical Gardening

The concept of vertical gardening and farming has emerged as a promising response to the challenge of land scarcity. Vertical gardening involves cultivating plants on vertically inclined surfaces such as walls, or up specifically formed vertical planting structures. Vertical farming takes this idea a step further by incorporating multi-level structures that allow for the cultivation of crops in stacked layers, often within controlled environments.

One noteworthy example comes from Singapore, a city known for its limited land resources. The country has embraced vertical farming as a means to enhance its food security. Sky Greens, a local vertical farm, uses a system of rotating tiers to maximise sunlight exposure for crops. This method not only optimises space but also significantly reduces the amount of water required for cultivation.

In Japan, the city of Kyoto has implemented innovative vertical gardening practices in urban areas. The Kyoto Botanical Gardens, for instance, showcase how vertical greenery can be seamlessly integrated into the urban landscape, not only providing aesthetic benefits but also contributing to biodiversity and improved air quality.

In the heart of the United States, the city of Chicago has embraced vertical farming with a focus on sustainability. The Plant, an old meat-packing facility turned vertical farm, uses a closed-loop system where waste from one part of the operation becomes a resource for another. This approach not only reduces environmental impact but also demonstrates the potential of circular economies in urban agriculture.

In Scandinavia, vertical gardening has been actively explored in the city of Stockholm as a means to incorporate green spaces into urban living. And the Bosco Verticale in Milan, Italy, stands as a globally renowned example of how vertical greenery can be seamlessly integrated into high-rise residential buildings. These towers host a variety of tree and plant species, creating a microcosm of biodiversity within the urban fabric.

Vertical gardening and farming often require less land and water than traditional horizontal farming. Moreover, the controlled environments in which vertical farming is often conducted allow for year-round cultivation, mitigating the seasonal constraints faced by conventional agriculture. Yet it's essential to approach these solutions with a critical eye. While vertical gardening and farming offer innovative ways to address land scarcity, they are not without challenges. Initial setup costs can be high, and the energy requirements for maintaining controlled environments may raise concerns about sustainability. Additionally, ensuring equitable access to these technologies is paramount if we are to avoid exacerbating social inequalities. Policies and initiatives that promote inclusivity and affordability should be at the forefront of urban development strategies. The future of generations living in urban environments is, therefore, intricately linked to our ability to address the challenges posed by land scarcity.

As we move forward, it's imperative to balance the enthusiasm for innovation with a thoughtful consideration of the environmental and social implications. Sustainable urban development requires not only technological advances but also inclusive policies that ensure the benefits of vertical gardening and farming reach all segments of the population. In doing so, in the future, we can pave the way for a more resilient and harmonious coexistence between urban environments and the natural world.

When it comes to conceptual ideas for the future of gardens and gardening there are a couple that stand out. The first is the idea of vertical forests and green roofs. Building on the success of vertical gardening, the concept of vertical forests takes it to a grand scale. Imagine entire skyscrapers covered in vegetation, contributing not only to aesthetics but also addressing urban air pollution. Green roofs on residential and commercial buildings could become more prevalent, providing insulation and creating urban oases. The result would be green vertical façades and green horizontal planes.

Augmented Reality

Alongside AI, the future might see the integration of Augmented Reality (AR) into gardening practices. Gardeners could use AR devices or apps to visualise potential garden layouts, identify plant species, and even receive real-time information about soil conditions. This would not only enhance the gardening experience but also serve as an educational tool.

The integration of AR into gardening represents a futuristic leap that promises to revolutionise the way individuals interact with and experience their outdoor spaces. AR holds immense potential for enhancing the gardening process, making it more interactive, educational and visually engaging – and, hopefully, fun! Imagine standing in your garden, holding up a tablet or wearing AR glasses, and seeing a holographic representation of your garden layout – we have started seeing this on TV gardening programmes. Augmented Reality can enable gardeners to visualise the placement of plants, pathways and features in real time, helping them make informed decisions about design and aesthetics. This interactive approach, therefore, enables gardeners to experiment with different layouts, plant combinations and hardscape features before making any physical changes, reducing the risk of costly mistakes. And, as holograms become more sophisticated in the future, we might even see the ability to physically interact with holographic images and videos, just like an episode of *Star Trek* in its holo-suite.

Augmented Reality technology can transform the way individuals identify plants. With a simple scan using a smartphone or AR device, users can access information about specific plants, including care instructions, ideal growing conditions and potential companions. This not only aids plant recognition but also serves as an educational tool for gardeners of all levels.

In addition, real-time guidance for gardening tasks can be given. For instance, a gardener wearing AR glasses could receive step-by-step instructions on how to properly prune a specific plant or when to water it based on soil moisture levels. Visual overlays could allow the gardener to see exactly where they need to cut and what will happen if they cut in the wrong place – in fact, at every step, a piece of relevant gardening information could be shared, downloaded in an instant, filed, shared with other gardeners, shared to social media and disseminated worldwide. Expert advice could be given, for example, by an orange grower based in California for a gardener/ user based in South Africa. I find it fascinating to know that companies are already exploring the development of AR gardening tools that overlay information onto the physical world. For example, an AR-enabled watering system can display a visual indicator when a plant needs watering or provide information about the amount of water required.

There are existing mobile phone applications out there, such as PlantSnap and PictureThis, which I use on a regular basis, and which harness recognition technology to identify plants from pictures taken by users. Augmented Reality could enhance these apps, going several steps further, allowing users to access 3D models of identified plants with additional information about care and maintenance in a 3D format that can be added, edited or discarded in real time and real space. Public gardens and botanical institutions could employ AR to create interactive and educational experiences for visitors. Augmented-Reality-enabled guided tours could provide information about plant species, their historical significance and ecological importance, enhancing the overall educational value of the visit. This is something that I have already been involved with, for a number of organisations, narrating a walk through an historic garden setting while talking about plants, plant combinations, the garden's history and its designers/protagonists. Aspiring gardeners could benefit from AR planting guides that offer visual cues for proper plant positioning, spacing, depth and companion planting.

While the concept of AR in gardening is exciting, it comes with challenges. The widespread adoption of AR gardening tools would require affordable and user-friendly hardware. Many people now have mobile phones, but as 'our lives' are held on our phones, how can we justify the expense of another portable device? Perhaps, in the future, the phone could also be our own personal AR device? Additionally, ensuring the accuracy of plant identification and gardening information is crucial to the success of such applications. With integrated AI, the AI bot will only disseminate the information that it finds on the internet, without any human fact checker or editor. How will we know if the information supplied is correct?

The integration of AR into gardening nevertheless holds immense potential for transforming the way people engage with their outdoor spaces. AR will enhance the interactive user experience. And, as technology continues to advance, we could anticipate a future where AR becomes an integral tool for both novice and experienced gardeners, fostering a deeper connection between gardeners and their gardens.

When it comes to the future, I think many people envisage a world run by robots – or should I say, more robots. The integration of robotics into gardening practices could revolutionise the way we maintain our outdoor spaces. This would not only save time but also enable more precise and efficient gardening practices.

Biophilic Design

In some senses, the future of gardening is already here, and it will be interesting to see how current schemes develop over the years. Here are a few examples:

- Singapore, a pioneer in urban gardening, has transformed itself into a 'City in a Garden'. The city-state actively promotes green spaces and vertical gardens. The Gardens by the Bay, featuring iconic 'Supertrees', is a prime example of how urban landscapes can be enhanced with a blend of technology and nature.

- Seattle's Beacon Food Forest is an innovative project that transforms a public space into an edible landscape. It incorporates fruit and nut trees, berries and herbs, creating a sustainable food source for the community. This concept of integrating edible plants into urban landscapes could become more widespread, promoting local food production, especially in light of the growth in food banks over recent years – good nutritious food without the food miles could be given out, improving the health and well-being of the community.

- The Netherlands, a global leader in agriculture, is home to high-tech greenhouses that use advanced technologies such as precision agriculture, climate control and automated systems. These green-houses allow for year-round cultivation and significantly reduce the environmental impact of traditional farming.

- The Amazon Spheres in Seattle represent a fusion of biophilic design and corporate spaces. These spherical conservatories house a diverse array of plant species, creating a unique working environment for Amazon employees. Biophilic design, integrating natural elements into architecture, could become a prevalent trend in urban development.

Biologist Edward O. Wilson coined the term '*biophilia*', proposing that humans have an inherent connection with the natural world. Biophilic design aims to enhance this connection by incorporating elements of nature into the built environment, complementing green architecture. The principles of biophilic design are rooted in the idea that exposure to nature, both directly and indirectly, has numerous benefits for human well-being. These principles can be applied to various spaces, including homes, offices, gardens and public areas.

Maximising the use of natural light and ventilation is a fundamental aspect of biophilic design. Large windows, skylights and open spaces allow for more sunlight and fresh air, creating a connection with the outside environment. Incorporating plants and greenery into spaces is a central element of biophilic design. Indoor gardens, potted plants and living walls not only enhance aesthetics but also contribute to improved air quality and overall well-being. In conjunction, the use of natural materials, like wood, stone and natural fabrics, helps create a sense of warmth and connection to the outdoors. These materials also have a lower environmental impact compared to synthetic alternatives. Designing spaces that attract and support wildlife, such as birds or butterflies, can further enhance the connection to nature. This could involve incorporating bird feeders, bat houses or native plantings.

Fundamental to designing spaces is to offer views of nature, whether it's a garden, water feature or landscape, providing a constant reminder of the natural world. Where green space is limited, particularly in urban environments, this can be incredibly beneficial. Integrating patterns and colours inspired by nature can also have a calming and positive impact. Earth tones, blues and greens are often used to mimic the colours found in natural surroundings. The inclusion of water features, such as fountains or reflecting pools, not only adds aesthetic value but also brings the soothing and calming qualities associated with water into the built environment. Creating dynamic and varied spaces – perhaps for movement, relaxation and social interaction – that mimic natural environments can stimulate creativity and improve overall well-being. Biophilic design has gained popularity in recent years as people recognise the positive impact it can have on mental health, productivity and overall satisfaction in the built environment. Architects, interior designers, garden designers and urban planners are increasingly incorporating these principles into their projects to create spaces that prioritise human well-being and environmental sustainability.

I very much hope that, in future, built environments will continue to follow the principles of biophilic design. How amazing it would be to wake up from a cryo-frozen state, three hundred years into the future, to see a greener urban environment, and a healthier world.

Mars is Calling

As you may have guessed by now, I'm a great sci-fi fan and I love the idea of leaving this planet to explore new worlds and new civilisations. The National Aeronautics and Space Administration (NASA)'s exploration of space extends beyond the confines of our planet, and the idea of gardening on different celestial bodies is a fascinating frontier. And while the idea of cultivating plants on distant planets is still largely theoretical, NASA has been actively engaged in research and experiments on Earth to understand the challenges and possibilities associated with extraterrestrial gardening.

The International Space Station (ISS) serves as a microgravity environment where NASA conducts various experiments, including those related to plant growth. NASA's Veggie experiment (launched in 2014), a plant growth chamber on the ISS, stands as a remarkable initiative that not only addresses the practical challenges of providing fresh food for astronauts but also contributes valuable insights into the future of space farming, life support systems for long-duration space missions and human habitation beyond Earth. This groundbreaking project, which successfully grew crops like lettuce and radishes, showcases the intersection of technology, agriculture and space exploration, offering a glimpse into the possibilities of sustainable cultivation in the unique microgravity environment of space and the future of off-world gardening.

One of the defining challenges of space farming is the adaptation of traditional agriculture to the microgravity environment of space. On Earth, plants rely on gravity to orient themselves properly for growth, but in space, this fundamental factor is absent. The Veggie experiment addresses this challenge by employing a unique system that allows plants to grow in a way that mimics Earth-like conditions as closely as possible. The growth chamber uses red, blue and green LED lights to stimulate plant growth through photosynthesis. These carefully calibrated lights provide the necessary spectrum for plants to undergo the process of converting light into energy, enabling them to grow and develop even in the absence of natural sunlight. This artificial light setup is crucial because, in the microgravity of space, plants cannot rely on the Sun's directional cues for growth.

Veggie has successfully cultivated various crop varieties on the ISS, showcasing the adaptability of certain plants to space conditions. In addition to the lettuce and radishes, mustard greens and zinnias have been grown successfully. These experiments not only serve as a proof of concept for growing edible plants in space but also contribute to the astronauts' diet, providing them with fresh and nutritious food during their missions.

The choice of lettuce as one of the primary crops is noteworthy. Apart from being a source of essential nutrients, lettuce has a short growth cycle and is well-suited for testing plant growth systems in microgravity. And, it has laid the foundation for considering a broader range of crops that could be cultivated on long-duration missions, where the availability of fresh, homegrown produce in astronauts' diet not only provides a source of essential vitamins and minerals but also contributes to their psychological well-being. The ability to nurture and harvest crops in space introduces a familiar element of terrestrial life, fostering a sense of connection to nature even in the most extraordinary environments. The Veggie experiment also serves an educational purpose, capturing the imagination of students and space enthusiasts worldwide. It provides a tangible example of the scientific and technological challenges that need to be overcome if sustained human exploration beyond Earth is to be achieved. By showcasing the process of growing crops in space, Veggie inspires the next generation of scientists, engineers and astronauts, fostering an interest in the intersection of space exploration and agriculture.

While Veggie's successes on the ISS are significant, the ultimate goal is to apply these lessons to future human missions to Mars. As humanity sets its sights on the Red Planet, the ability to cultivate food in space becomes a critical component of ensuring the well-being and sustainability of future Mars colonists. Despite the successes, challenges persist in the endeavour to establish sustainable space farming systems. The limitations of space, including restricted resources, energy constraints and the need for efficient recycling systems, necessitate ongoing research and innovation. Future developments may involve exploring more crop varieties, refining growth systems and addressing the complexities of closed-loop life support systems.

In order to see if horticultural and agricultural techniques can be undertaken in space and even on Mars, there are several testing grounds on Earth. The first that comes to mind is the Mars Desert Research Station (MDRS), operated by the Mars Society in Utah, USA. It's a terrestrial analogue site designed to simulate the conditions of Mars. Researchers and space enthusiasts at MDRS engage in experiments related to plant growth, testing different cultivation techniques and technologies that might be applicable to Martian environments. The GreenHab facility at MDRS allows for controlled experiments in plant biology. Next is NASA's collaboration with institutions like the Fairchild Tropical Botanic Garden in Miami for initiatives like the Growing Beyond Earth Challenge. This challenge encourages students to design and experiment with plant growth systems that could potentially be deployed on future space missions. It fosters creativity and innovation in space farming. NASA's terrestrial efforts extend to the Hawaii Space Exploration Analog and Simulation (HI-SEAS) programme. Analogue missions, which simulate the conditions of space exploration on Earth, include studies on growing food in confined spaces, contributing valuable data to future space farming initiatives.

While not directly related to gardening, NASA's Perseverance rover on Mars includes an instrument called MOXIE (Mars Oxygen In-Situ Resource Utilization Experiment). MOXIE aims to produce oxygen from the carbon dioxide in Mars' atmosphere, showcasing the potential for utilising local resources during future human missions and, indirectly, for potential gardening efforts. While the dream of gardening on different planets remains a futuristic vision, NASA's experiments on Earth and aboard the ISS contribute significantly to our understanding of the challenges and possibilities associated with extraterrestrial cultivation. As technology advances and humanity looks towards future missions to Mars and beyond, the insights gained from these experiments will play a crucial role in developing sustainable solutions for space exploration.

Of course, gardening on Mars presents a fascinating prospect beyond terrestrial horticulture's traditional boundaries. Mars poses numerous challenges for plant growth, including extreme temperatures, low atmospheric pressure and high radiation levels. Designing a gardening system that can withstand these harsh conditions is a crucial consideration. Mars also has limited resources such as water and nutrient-rich soil. Developing efficient and sustainable methods for resource utilisation, recycling and conservation is imperative if gardening on Mars is to be successful. The lack of natural sunlight necessitates the use of artificial lighting for plant growth. Designing systems that provide the right spectrum and intensity of light for photosynthesis will be essential. The lower gravity could have unknown effects on plant growth. Bioregenerative life support systems may involve creating a closed-loop environment where plants, humans and other organisms interact to maintain a sustainable ecosystem. This approach aims to recycle waste products into resources for plant growth, creating a self-sustaining cycle.

Future gardening techniques will need to be considered if these challenges are to be surmounted. They may include implementing Controlled Environment Agriculture (CEA), such as hydroponics or aeroponics. These soil-less systems allow for precise control of nutrient delivery and environmental conditions, mitigating the challenges associated with Martian soil. Genetic modification may be needed to enhance plants' adaptability to Martian and other planetary conditions. Scientists could explore modifying plant genomes to make them more resilient to extreme temperatures, radiation and nutrient deficiencies. Developing advanced lighting systems using LEDs or other technologies may provide the necessary light spectrum for plant growth on Mars. These systems would need to be energy-efficient and tailored to the specific needs of plants in a Martian environment.

The prospect of gardening on Mars is not only about providing sustenance for potential future Martian colonies but also about creating a semblance of Earth's ecosystems in an otherwise inhospitable environment. Beyond the technical and scientific challenges, successful Martian gardening could have profound psychological benefits for future space travellers, providing a connection to the natural cycles of growth and life. As we continue to advance our understanding of both Martian conditions and plant biology, the dream of cultivating gardens on Mars moves from science fiction to a plausible reality. While significant hurdles remain, the intersection of technology, biology and space exploration holds the promise of turning the barren landscapes of Mars into thriving, green habitats for future generations.

ı ⟩ ⟩ ⟩ ⟩ ⟩

Of course, it's not just Mars that is capturing the minds of scientists, biologists, horticulturalists and engineers. Gardening on other planets remains a speculative yet intriguing concept that pushes the boundaries of human exploration and habitation. While the notion of cultivating plants on celestial bodies beyond Earth is primarily rooted in future aspirations, various other worldwide examples and research initiatives contribute valuable insights and inspiration to this futuristic endeavour.

The Moon, with its harsh conditions, presents another challenge for potential gardening. The powdery soil-like substance on the Moon's surface poses unique challenges and opportunities. Research into growing plants in simulated lunar soil, known as *lunar regolith simulant*, provides insights into the complexities of gardening in low-gravity environments.

The lunar environment is hostile and markedly different from Earth, presenting unique challenges for any form of plant cultivation. The Moon experiences extreme temperature variations, ranging from scorching heat during lunar daytime to frigid cold during the night. Plants would need to withstand these temperature extremes to thrive. There is a lack of substantial atmosphere, which means there is no protection from solar radiation and micrometeoroids. This lack of atmosphere poses a challenge for the development and protection of delicate plant life. Additionally, the absence of liquid water on the Moon complicates traditional irrigation methods.

China's Chang'e-4 mission marked a historic milestone in lunar exploration and inadvertently became a pioneer in lunar gardening. Launched in 2018, the mission included a lunar lander and rover that successfully landed on the far side of the Moon, specifically in the Von Kármán crater. As part of the mission, a small, sealed biosphere containing cotton seeds, rapeseed, potato and *arabidopsis* (a small flowering plant related to cabbage and mustard) was included. This biosphere, known as the Lunar Micro Ecosystem (LME), aimed to test the possibility of plant growth in the challenging lunar environment. The cotton seeds successfully germinated and sprouted, making history as the first plants to grow on the Moon's surface. However, the experiment was short-lived due to the extreme conditions, and the cotton plants didn't survive the subsequent lunar night, which lasts for approximately two weeks.

There are several key lessons to be learnt from China's lunar experiment. The successful germination of cotton seeds demonstrated that, under controlled conditions, plants could initiate growth on the lunar surface. The inability of the plants to survive the extended lunar night highlighted the challenges associated with temperature extremes and the absence of sunlight. In addition, the experiment highlighted the importance of controlled environments and life support systems for sustaining plant life on the Moon. Future lunar gardening endeavours would likely involve using enclosed habitats or greenhouses equipped with artificial lighting and climate control systems.

While the initial lunar gardening experiments have provided valuable insights, the path forward involves addressing the identified challenges and advancing the technology needed for sustained plant growth on the Moon. Some key considerations for future lunar gardening endeavours include:

- Designing enclosed habitats or greenhouses that shield plants from harsh lunar conditions while providing controlled environments with appropriate lighting, temperature and nutrients;
- Developing technologies for using local resources, such as regolith, for plant growth. This includes exploring ways to extract essential nutrients and minerals from lunar soil to support plant development;
- Integrating lunar gardening into broader bio-regenerative life support systems, where plants contribute to the production of oxygen, removal of carbon dioxide and recycling of nutrients within a closed-loop environment; and

- Researching and adapting terrestrial plant species to thrive in lunar conditions. Genetic modification and selective breeding may play a role in developing lunar-tailored plant varieties.

Elsewhere, the European Space Agency (ESA) leads the Micro-Ecological Life Support System Alternative (MELiSSA) project. This initiative aims to develop closed-loop life support systems, including plant cultivation, for long-duration space missions. While not specifically focused on extraterrestrial gardening, MELiSSA provides essential knowledge for sustainable life support in space. Established in 1975, the ESA is an intergovernmental organisation dedicated to the exploration of space. With twenty-two member states, the agency collaborates on a wide range of space-related projects, including Earth observation, satellite development, human space flight and planetary exploration. The ESA stands at the forefront of space exploration, scientific research and technological innovation. While the agency has not specifically conducted missions centred around gardening in space or on other planets, its broader initiatives in space science, life support systems and sustainable habitation contribute to the foundational knowledge needed for future extraterrestrial gardening endeavours.

The European Space Agency's systems are crucial for maintaining air quality, recycling waste and providing essential resources for extended space missions. Again, while not directly tied to planetary gardening, the ESA's European Modular Cultivation System (EMCS) is designed to study plant growth in microgravity conditions. EMCS allows researchers to investigate the effects of space conditions on plant development, providing insights into potential challenges and solutions for extraterrestrial cultivation.

In collaboration with Roscosmos, the Russian space agency, the ESA has been a major partner in the ExoMars programme. While focused on robotic exploration, the mission lays the groundwork for potential human missions to Mars. Understanding the Martian environment is critical for envisioning future gardening efforts on the Red Planet. The development of space greenhouses and bioregenerative life support systems is an area where Roscosmos has shown interest. These systems aim to create self-sustaining environments where plants contribute to the recycling of waste and the generation of oxygen. Roscosmos has also conducted plant growth experiments on the ISS as part of the LADA experiment (LADA stands for 'greenhouse' in Russian). LADA aims to study the effects of microgravity on plant growth. This experiment involves growing various plant species in a controlled environment to understand how microgravity influences plant development.

Established in 2003, the Japan Aerospace Exploration Agency (JAXA) has significantly advanced Japan's space capabilities. The agency has been involved in various missions, including planetary exploration, satellite launches and participation in the ISS programme. JAXA's Kibo module has hosted experiments investigating space agriculture. Researchers have explored different aspects of plant growth, including the effects of microgravity on germination, development and the overall health of various plant species.

All this work, undertaken by scientists and engineers around the world, is truly fascinating: it has captured my imagination, and will affect how I think, digest and disseminate my horticultural knowledge in the future. If humans are to reach other planets, plants will undoubtedly play an important role. Yet we still need to fully understand the role of plants and fungi right here on Earth. I recently watched a sci-fi TV series where algae were instrumental to the health of a spacecraft and its inhabitants. What we see in sci-fi TV series and movies is, most of the time, based on fact or scientific hypothesis. So, the next time you watch something based in space and see plants of any description, remember that somewhere on this planet, scientists, possibly from NASA or the ESA, are probably researching the use of those plants in space right now.

The Power
of Plants

Throughout this book I have mentioned the importance of community, communication and the sharing
of knowledge. I therefore felt it was important to write
something about the intricate language of botany,
or the silent conversations of plants. For millions
of years, plants have existed on our planet; humans
are the number one predator when it comes to land
acquisition and environmental destruction. Perhaps if
we all knew a little bit more about plants and how
they talk to each other, we could learn something new
and help turn back the clock on climate change and
the rape and destruction of our planet.

In the quiet realms of nature there is a silent
symphony unfolding. It's a form of communication
not conducted through spoken words or audible

signals, but rather through a subtle exchange of biochemical cues and intricate responses. This phenomenon involves the complex interplay of plants conversing with each other, signalling and reacting to their surroundings in ways that have captivated the curiosity of scientists and nature enthusiasts alike. The traditional perception of plants as static, passive organisms has undergone a transformative shift as scientific research has unravelled the sophisticated ways in which they communicate. The botanical language, although devoid of words, is rich in chemical signals and responses that facilitate a dynamic interaction among plants. At the heart of this communication lies an intricate web of mechanisms that enable plants to convey information about their well-being, environmental conditions and potential threats.

One of the primary modes of botanical communication involves the release of volatile organic compounds (VOCs). These are a diverse array of chemicals emitted by plants into the air, creating a biochemical language that neighbouring plants can interpret. VOCs serve as messengers, transmitting information about the plant's health, its stress levels and even its encounters with herbivores or pathogens. When a plant faces a threat, such as an insect attack, it releases specific VOCs as a distress signal. These compounds can alert nearby plants, enabling them to pre-emptively activate defence mechanisms. This phenomenon, known as 'indirect plant defence', demonstrates how plants can mobilise their natural defences in response to the distress signals emitted by their neighbours.

Detecting VOCs emitted by plants requires specialised equipment designed to capture, analyse and quantify these chemical compounds. The first is gas chromatography. It's a widely used analytical technique. A sample is vapourised and injected into a chromatograph. The compounds travel through a column and are separated based on their chemical properties. A detector then analyses the separated compounds, producing a chromatogram. It's effective for identifying and quantifying a wide range of VOCs emitted by plants.

Anyone who watches crime series on TV, especially with crime-scene investigation as part of the storyline, will probably have heard of mass spectrometry. It's often coupled with gas chromatography to enhance the identification of volatile compounds. Compounds separated by gas chromatography are ionised, and the resulting ions are analysed based on their mass-to-charge ratio. This provides precise identification of individual compounds. Proton transfer reaction mass spectrometry (PTR-MS) is a high-sensitivity mass spectrometric technique for detecting trace gases. VOCs are ionised by proton transfer, and the resulting ions are analysed in real time. It's particularly useful for continuous, online monitoring of plant emissions, offering high sensitivity and temporal resolution. Like sensors that can detect rainfall, etc., gas sensors are available for detecting specific VOCs or classes of compounds. Gas sensors are based on diverse technologies, such as metal-oxide semiconductors, conducting polymers or surface acoustic wave devices. They respond to changes in the concentration of specific VOCs. Gas sensors are suitable for continuous monitoring, especially in field settings where real-time data is crucial.

Next, solid-phase microextraction (SPME) is a sampling technique that extracts VOCs from the air or a sample matrix. A fibre coated with a sorbent material is exposed to the air or sample, adsorbing VOCs. The fibre is then inserted into a gas chromatograph for analysis. It's used for sampling VOCs in the air around plants or directly from plant tissues.

I love the world of bioluminescence, the production and emission of light by living organisms, and although it's not the same, fluorescence spectroscopy really excites me, as it measures the fluorescence emitted by certain compounds, including some VOCs. When excited by specific wavelengths of light, certain VOCs fluoresce, and this fluorescence is measured to determine their presence and concentration.

Emission Collection Systems are specialised systems designed to collect VOC emissions directly from plants. Enclosures or chambers are placed around plant parts, and the emitted gases are collected using sorbent tubes or other trapping mechanisms. These systems are useful for studying the emission patterns of specific plant organs or under controlled conditions. Infrared Gas Analysers (IRGA) measure the absorption of infrared radiation by gases, including certain VOCs. Infrared light is passed through a gas sample, and the amount of absorbed light is correlated with the concentration of specific gases. They are often used for real-time monitoring of CO_2 and other gases, and adaptations can be made for specific VOCs.

When conducting research on plant VOC emissions, scientists often employ a combination of these techniques to gain a comprehensive understanding of the volatile compounds released by plants. The choice of equipment depends on the specific objectives of the study, the type of VOCs of interest and the required sensitivity and precision of the analysis. This is where science is changing our perception about the plant world. We have only been able to understand these compounds in the last eighty years, and as scientific devices and machines become more sophisticated, who knows what the future will hold for our understanding of the mechanisms of plant life.

ı)))))

Below the soil's surface, an intricate network of *mycorrhizal* fungi serves as an underground communication highway for plants. Mycorrhizae form symbiotic relationships with plant roots, facilitating nutrient exchange. Remarkably, these networks also allow plants to share information. Studies have revealed that when a plant is under stress, it can release chemical signals into the soil, which are then picked up by mycorrhizal networks. These networks, acting as conduits for communication, transmit the information to neighbouring plants. This form of 'root-to-root' communication enables plants to warn each other about impending threats, creating a system reminiscent of a botanical alarm network.

Arbuscular mycorrhizal fungi are the most common type of mycorrhizal fungi, forming a symbiotic relationship with about 80 per cent of plant species, including many garden plants. They assist in nutrient absorption, particularly of phosphorus, by extending their *hyphae* (collectively known as *mycelium*) into the soil and increasing the surface area for nutrient uptake. Consider a vegetable garden where crops like tomatoes, beans or peas establish a strong symbiotic mycorrhizal association. The fungi help these plants access essential nutrients, leading to healthier and more robust growth. Next are *ectomycorrhizal* fungi, which are commonly associated with trees, especially conifers and hardwoods. These fungi form a dense network around the plant roots, creating a protective barrier and aiding in nutrient exchange, particularly of nitrogen and phosphorus. In a woodland garden, for example, with a variety of trees such as oaks, birches or pines, the presence of ectomycorrhizal fungi fosters a healthier and more resilient ecosystem. The fungi contribute to the overall vitality of each tree and of the trees as a collective, as well as of understorey plants.

Ericoid mycorrhizal fungi specialise in forming associations with plants from the heath family, such as rhododendrons and heathers. They play a crucial role in nutrient uptake, especially of nitrogen, and contribute to the adaptation of plants to acidic soils. Imagine a garden with a vibrant collection of heather plants. The presence of ericoid mycorrhizal fungi in the soil helps these plants thrive in acidic conditions, enhancing their colour and overall health.

Orchids, known for their intricate beauty, and loved by many, often rely on specific *orchid mycorrhizal fungi* for germination and early growth. The fungi assist orchid seeds in germination, providing necessary nutrients until the plants can establish photosynthesis. In an orchid enthusiast's garden, for example, the reliance on orchid mycorrhizal fungi is evident in the successful cultivation of diverse orchid species. The fungi contribute significantly to the early stages of orchid development.

The symbiotic relationship between plants and mycorrhizal fungi enriches the soil with essential nutrients, promoting healthy plant growth. Mycorrhizal fungi can enhance a plant's resistance to diseases, contributing to a more robust and resilient garden ecosystem. The extensive network of fungal hyphae improves soil structure, increasing water retention and aeration. Therefore, mycorrhizal fungi are integral to the success of garden ecosystems, enhancing the vitality of plants and contributing to a sustainable and thriving environment. By understanding and harnessing the power of these fungi, gardeners can create gardens that not only captivate us with their beauty but also flourish in a harmonious relationship with nature.

In addition to signalling distress or threats, plants engage in chemical interactions that influence the growth and development of nearby vegetation. This phenomenon, known as *allelopathy*, involves the release of biochemical compounds that can either inhibit or stimulate the growth of neighbouring plants. Certain plant species produce allelopathic chemicals to suppress the growth of competitors, gaining a competitive advantage in resource utilisation. Black walnut trees, for example, release *juglone*, a chemical that inhibits the growth of many plants around them. On the other hand, some plants release allelopathic compounds to foster symbiotic relationships with specific species, showcasing a nuanced and strategic employment of chemical communication.

While the intricate language of plants involves signalling to one another, plants are also remarkably adept at perceiving and responding to their environment. Understanding how plants react to external stimuli is essential in unravelling the depth of their communication abilities. Plants exhibit fascinating responses to light and gravity, known as *phototropism* and *gravitropism* respectively. Phototropism involves the bending of plant parts towards a light source, ensuring optimal light absorption for photosynthesis. This responsiveness allows plants to adapt to changing light conditions and compete for sunlight. Gravitropism, on the other hand, dictates how plants orient themselves in response to gravity. Roots typically exhibit positive gravitropism, growing towards the gravitational pull, while shoots display negative gravitropism, growing away from it. These tropic responses enable plants to navigate their environment, optimising their growth and development.

Plants are also capable of responding to touch through a phenomenon known as *thigmotropism*. This tactile sensitivity allows plants to detect physical contact and adjust their growth accordingly. For instance, climbing plants such as vines may alter their growth patterns in response to the touch of a nearby support structure, ensuring stability and efficient climbing.

Beyond the realm of volatile compounds and tropic responses, plants exhibit a rapid form of communication through electrochemical signalling. When a plant encounters a stressor, such as herbivore feeding or pathogen attack, it can initiate an electrical signal that travels through its tissues. This signal, often referred to as an 'action potential', triggers the release of signalling molecules like calcium ions. The rapid transmission of electrical signals enables plants to mount a swift and coordinated response to threats, showcasing an intricacy in communication that extends beyond the slower diffusion of VOCs.

While scientific advances have provided insights into the remarkable ways in which plants communicate and react to their surroundings, decoding the entirety of this botanical language remains a challenge. Perhaps the future of gardening will find a way to decode these mysteries; I very much hope so. The complexity of plant communication systems, the diversity of plant species and the multifaceted nature of environmental interactions create a rich tapestry that scientists are continuously unravelling.

The burgeoning field of plant communication holds implications that extend beyond the realm of scientific curiosity. Understanding how plants communicate and respond to their environment has practical applications in agriculture, ecology and even the potential development of sustainable technologies. In the realm of agriculture, insights into plant communication can revolutionise crop management strategies. By deciphering the chemical signals emitted by plants under stress, farmers may be able to detect pest infestations or diseases at an early stage. This early warning system could enable targeted interventions, reducing reliance on chemical pesticides and promoting more sustainable agricultural practices. In other words, farmers can alter their farming practices because they understand plant communication. Moreover, the understanding of allelopathic interactions between plants opens avenues for designing crop rotations that capitalise on the natural growth-stimulating or inhibitory effects of specific plant species. This knowledge could contribute to the development of more resilient and productive agricultural systems.

Knowledge of plant communication can inform strategies for restoring degraded ecosystems. By selecting plant species that exhibit positive allelopathic interactions or symbiotic relationships through mycorrhizal networks, restoration ecologists can enhance the success of reforestation projects and the recovery of biodiversity. Inspired by the efficiency of plant communication and responsiveness to environmental stimuli, researchers are currently exploring applications in green technologies. The integration of plant-inspired sensors and bio-hybrid systems could lead to innovative solutions in environmental monitoring, where living plants serve as biological sensors capable of detecting changes in air quality, pollution levels or even the presence of specific substances. This exploration of bio-hybrid systems represents a cutting-edge avenue in the realm of environmental monitoring, offering innovative solutions that seamlessly integrate living organisms with technology to enhance our understanding of ecosystems. This approach holds immense promise in addressing the complex challenges associated with environmental monitoring, providing real-time insights and sustainable solutions.

What are known as bio-hybrid systems involve the integration of biological components, such as plants, microbes or animals, with artificial sensors and monitoring devices. This integration enables the monitoring of environmental parameters in a dynamic and responsive manner, as living organisms can act as natural sensors that respond to changes in their surroundings. For example, the use of plants as environmental sensors, a technique known as 'plant nanobionics', is gaining ground. Researchers have developed plants with embedded nanoparticles that can detect pollutants or changes in soil moisture, providing valuable data for environmental monitoring.

Living sensors can contribute to the monitoring of air quality by utilising the sensitivity of living organisms to pollutants. For instance, moss-covered walls in urban areas can serve as living air quality sensors. Moss has a high affinity for heavy metals and air pollutants, and changes in its health can indicate variations in air quality. The CityTree project in cities like Berlin and London uses bio-hybrid systems incorporating moss cultures in urban installations to monitor and improve air quality. These installations act as both aesthetic elements and effective environmental sensors.

Aquatic bio-hybrid systems can be employed to monitor water quality and detect contaminants. Combining electronic sensors with aquatic organisms, such as fish or algae, allows for real-time monitoring of parameters like water temperature, pH levels and the presence of pollutants. The Smart Fin project, developed by the Surfrider Foundation and Scripps Institution of Oceanography, USA, involves attaching sensor-equipped fins to marine animals, turning them into mobile data collectors. This bio-hybrid approach allows for the collection of valuable information about ocean conditions, contributing to marine conservation efforts.

Innovations based on current and future scientific understanding can revolutionise soil monitoring by using the natural capabilities of plants and microbes. Incorporating microbial fuel cells into the soil allows for the generation of electrical signals in response to changes in soil conditions. This can be coupled with plant-based sensors to create a comprehensive monitoring system. The Plant-e system, developed in the Netherlands, uses living plants to generate electricity through microbial processes in the soil. This sustainable approach not only monitors soil conditions but also provides a renewable energy source.

Bio-hybrid systems, therefore, enable continuous, real-time data collection, offering a more accurate representation of environmental conditions compared to traditional monitoring methods. By harnessing the natural capabilities of living organisms, these systems can contribute to sustainable and eco-friendly monitoring solutions. Bio-hybrid systems can adapt to changes in the environment, providing a flexible and responsive monitoring infrastructure. Therefore, such systems represent a transformative approach to environmental monitoring, fostering a deeper understanding of ecosystems while offering sustainable and innovative solutions.

Conclusion

Whatever the future holds for gardening, I strongly believe that humans will be the instigators of change, while technology, AI and AR will assist. Will AI take over the world? Who knows? If we look at the natural world, we know that there have been five mass extinctions in the history of Earth. Perhaps human-kind's extinction will be number six. Our planet will then be left to AI and robots to carry on our practices. In time, we shall be forgotten, but AI will remember that its knowledge came predominantly from us, through our stories throughout history, our scientific exploration and discoveries, our historical records and our knowledge that we've passed down through the generations. It might even get to a point when Earth is left completely to the natural world, as we or our future robotic selves delve into space in search of other life-forms. I actually get a warm sensation when I think Earth could become a utopian planet, overrun by nature. The natural world would find its own balance once again.

I know this all sounds a bit 'doom and gloom', but even with accelerating technological advancement, I think it will be some time before we reach the above point. As a gardener and garden designer, I think the prospects for gardening in the near future are exciting. As we learn more about the natural world, how various life-forms communicate with each other and how we can monitor and alter our practices, based on what we've learnt from plants, for the benefit of mankind, I do really think that we can improve our physical and mental, and for some their spiritual well-being.

I do wonder what life will be like when my great-nieces and their children are my age, but I hope that my skills and knowledge will help them navigate the world while still reaping the benefits of gardening. For now, however, I shall continue to design outdoor spaces that are accessible and inclusive.

Before I sign off, I want to cover accessibility and inclusivity, especially on a personal level. As the UK's first garden designer who uses a wheelchair all the time, I have come up against many obstacles. Yet I'm a strong believer that thinking outside of the box can really help. Now, none of us has a crystal ball. Who knows what ailments or disabilities we may get as we age? We are an ageing population, and, unfortunately, as we get older, we might start to ache in places that we never thought existed before. When designing a garden, I ask clients three very pertinent questions right at the start:

- First, how long do you intend to stay in your home, i.e. is it your forever home?
- Second, do you have a disability?
- And third, whether they answer yes or no, do they want the garden to be an adaptable space, without it looking institutional?

I often get strange looks when I ask these questions, but it's imperative that we learn not only our clients' wishes for their outdoor space but also how they intend to use it in future years.

None of us is getting any younger, but that doesn't mean we should be banished to the sofa with a remote in our hands, only getting up to pop to the toilet or to make ourselves something to eat. We know gardening, gardens and green spaces improve our well-being both physically and mentally. I know that as soon as I get outside; I feel the stresses of modern life lifting and my eye starts to see what needs to be done. There are times when I just stop and look at the planting combinations, the spaces created in and around the plants, and the wildlife that they attract, but being a very keen gardener there is always something to do.

When people start hearing or reading that adaptations need to be made for disabled gardeners or for the elderly, visions of concrete ramps, ugly railings, raised beds and tired or unusable spaces come to mind – well, they do for me. There are, of course, some very good examples and these should be applauded. But, alas, I've seen many gardens which have been 'adapted', where quite honestly the designer or company involved should spend a day in a wheelchair and see how difficult supposedly easy tasks can become.

Designing gardens or landscapes for accessibility should really be about designing for inclusivity, so that anyone can enjoy the space no matter their level of ability or disability. The aim should always be to provide inclusive design and, through that, achieve social inclusion. Inclusive design is also not a fixed set of design criteria but an evolving attitude that results in aesthetically pleasing and functional environments that can be used by everyone. My hope is that gardens or outdoor spaces in the future will naturally be designed with inclusivity at the core, without it having to be a 'considered' at all.

The term 'disability' is broad, and includes people living with physical, sensory or mental issues; it is estimated that between 12 and 13 per cent of the population have some degree of impairment. While many aspects of design will be helpful to all or most people with disabilities, specific design considerations are also needed for those with a particular disability. Therefore, it's important to consider individuals' own impairment or disability, requirements, needs and aspirations, just as you would for any design. It's essential to understand the disability. Ask questions about:

- The weight of a wheelchair, its size, the height of footplates and knee height, eye height (on average between 960mm and 1,315mm), seat height, the width of the tyres, the size of the front wheels;
- How far can the person reach?
- Can they twist their torso or arms or are they restricted?
- Do they have difficulty with proprioception, i.e. knowing where their limbs and body are in relation to the environment around them?
- Are they visually impaired or blind?

The more questions the better. This will build a complete picture – and remember that disabilities change as people get older, just as physical changes occur for ambulant people, so time also needs to be considered.

⊢ ⊦ ▸ ▸ ▶ ▶

Gardens are getting smaller, and as more of us live in urban environments, space will be at a premium. Futuristic renderings depict vertical living with no outdoor spaces, so it needs to be remembered that the size of your garden doesn't matter; you can still create a stress-free environment that can offer *restoration*. It's also important to remember that not just the outside space but also the indoor space can be filled with plants. Bringing nature into our homes by introducing houseplants has a biophilic effect on us. Group plants together to create lush compositions, especially in areas where you sit and relax. Looking at something green, such as a house-plant, will help slow our heart rate, make us feel more relaxed, and help lift anxiety and depression while also contributing to better quality of air. Over the last fifty years, the proportion of the population living in urban environments has increased by 20 per cent, and that is set to increase as our world becomes more and more developed. However, we are beginning to understand how and why we can get so much peace and well-being from nature and what we can do to improve our own lives.

We have long believed that being outside and connecting to nature has a positive effect on us, whether biologically, reducing stress responses and lowering blood pressure, emotionally, reducing the effects of depression or anxiety, or simply making us feel more able to cope with the daily challenges that we face in our modern lives. Proving this has always been tricky, but research is continuously being published on the subject. Who knows what we'll find out in the future?

As previously mentioned, one of the main concepts we often refer to when considering the positive effect nature has on ourselves, is biophilia, a term that was first used in 1973 and in a paper by a Harvard scientist in 1984. It noted that 'Peaceful or nurturing elements of nature, helped us regain equanimity, cognitive clarity, empathy and hope'.

It was also noted that those of us that were most attuned to cues from nature were the ones who survived to pass on those traits. In other words, we evolved in nature, so we are evolutionarily linked to nature, and to its effect on us and subsequent generations. 'Biophilia' is therefore used when talking about the positive and restorative effect that nature can have on us. There is an innately emotional connection of human beings to other living things. It helps us to understand how people are motivated to interact with nature and gardening and gain their healing benefits. The term 'restoration' is often used as an idea that we're 'healed' or that we can 'recover' after spending time in nature. I think we can all relate to the calming feeling we get when we walk through a park or woodland or spend some time in the countryside – this is restoration.

As we learn more about plants, strive for an inclusive society, for the betterment of all mankind and our planet, I hope – no, I know – that gardens and gardening will always be a part of our lives, forever!

Acknowledgements

I want to thank Tom Clayton from Melville House Publishing, without whom this book would not have happened. I also thank Tom for his wit, insightful comments and his 'not-so-deaf white cat'. I also thank my agent, Andrew Roach from Insanity, without whom my sanity would sometimes be questioned. Steve Gove for his copyediting and remarks, which magically made my sentences and paragraphs make sense when very little else did.

My husband, Jasen Cavalli, has put up with late nights and stressed mornings; I would like to thank him from the bottom of my heart.

I applaud the incredible work being undertaken across our wonderful planet by international space agencies, climate activists, farmers, environmentalists,

ecologists, climatologists, hydrologists, horticulturalists, pedologists, edaphologists and soil scientists
– as well as those astronauts and scientists who are
looking to the stars.

To us gardeners who are already adapting to our
ever-changing climate to become resilient gardeners, constantly looking to improve biodiversity and
sustainability on both a micro and a macro level. To
the plants themselves, which have the power within
them to make change.

Finally, to NASA. This is not so much a direct
acknowledgement as a wish: to take me on the jour-
ney to Mars and beyond!

… And, of course, to anyone that I've missed.

About the Series

Each volume in the FUTURES Series presents a vision imagined by an accomplished writer and subject expert. The series seeks to publish a diverse range of voices, covering as wide-ranging a view as possible of our potential prospects. Inspired by the brilliant 'To-Day and To-Morrow' books from a century ago, we ask our authors to write in a spirit of pragmatic hope, and with a commitment to map out potential future landscapes, highlighting both beauties and dangers. We hope the books in the FUTURES Series will inspire readers to imagine what might lie ahead, to figure out how they might like the future to look, and, indeed, to think about how we might get there.

The FUTURES Series was originally conceived by Professor Max Saunders and Dr Lisa Gee, both of whom work at the University of Birmingham. Saunders is Interdisciplinary Professor of Modern Literature and Culture, author of *Imagined Futures: Writing, Science, and Modernity in the To-Day and To-Morrow book series*, 1923–31 (OUP 2019), and editor of *The To-day and To-morrow Reader* (Routledge, 2024), and Gee is Assistant Professor in Creative Writing and Digital Media and Research Fellow in Future Thinking.

To find out more about their Future Thinking work visit www.birmingham.ac.uk/futures

Also available in the FUTURES Series: